W9-CAX-512

COMPREHENSIVE RESEARCH
AND STUDY GUIDE

BLOOM'S
MAJOR
SHORT
STORY
WRITERS

Ernest
Hemingway

EDITED AND WITH AN
INTRODUCTION BY HAROLD BLOOM

BLOOM'S MAJOR DRAMATISTS

Anton Chekhov
Henrik Ibsen
Arthur Miller
Eugene O'Neill
Shakespeare's Comedies
Shakespeare's Histories
Shakespeare's Romances
Shakespeare's Tragedies
George Bernard Shaw
Tennessee Williams

BLOOM'S MAJOR NOVELISTS

Jane Austen
The Brontës
Willa Cather
Charles Dickens
William Faulkner
F. Scott Fitzgerald
Nathaniel Hawthorne
Ernest Hemingway
Toni Morrison
John Steinbeck
Mark Twain
Alice Walker

BLOOM'S MAJOR SHORT STORY WRITERS

William Faulkner
F. Scott Fitzgerald
Ernest Hemingway
O. Henry
James Joyce
Herman Melville
Flannery O'Connor
Edgar Allan Poe
J. D. Salinger
John Steinbeck
Mark Twain
Eudora Welty

BLOOM'S MAJOR WORLD POETS

Geoffrey Chaucer
Emily Dickinson
John Donne
T. S. Eliot
Robert Frost
Langston Hughes
John Milton
Edgar Allan Poe
Shakespeare's Poems & Sonnets
Alfred, Lord Tennyson
Walt Whitman
William Wordsworth

BLOOM'S NOTES

The Adventures of Huckleberry Finn
Aeneid
The Age of Innocence
Animal Farm
The Autobiography of Malcolm X
The Awakening
Beloved
Beowulf
Billy Budd, Benito Cereno, & Bartleby the Scrivener
Brave New World
The Catcher in the Rye
Crime and Punishment
The Crucible

Death of a Salesman
A Farewell to Arms
Frankenstein
The Grapes of Wrath
Great Expectations
The Great Gatsby
Gulliver's Travels
Hamlet
Heart of Darkness & The Secret Sharer
Henry IV, Part One
I Know Why the Caged Bird Sings
Iliad
Inferno
Invisible Man
Jane Eyre
Julius Caesar

King Lear
Lord of the Flies
Macbeth
A Midsummer Night's Dream
Moby-Dick
Native Son
Nineteen Eighty-Four
Odyssey
Oedipus Plays
Of Mice and Men
The Old Man and the Sea
Othello
Paradise Lost
A Portrait of the Artist as a Young Man
The Portrait of a Lady

Pride and Prejudice
The Red Badge of Courage
Romeo and Juliet
The Scarlet Letter
Silas Marner
The Sound and the Fury
The Sun Also Rises
A Tale of Two Cities
Tess of the D'Urbervilles
Their Eyes Were Watching God
To Kill a Mockingbird
Uncle Tom's Cabin
Wuthering Heights

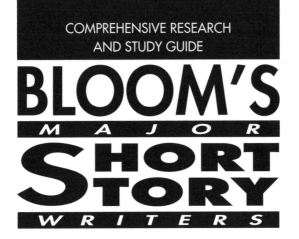

COMPREHENSIVE RESEARCH
AND STUDY GUIDE

BLOOM'S
MAJOR
SHORT
STORY
WRITERS

Ernest
Hemingway

EDITED AND WITH AN INTRODUCTION BY HAROLD BLOOM

© 1999 by Chelsea House Publishers, a subsidiary of Haights Cross Communications.

Introduction © 1999 by Harold Bloom

Printed and bound in the United States of America.

3 5 7 9 8 6 4

Library of Congress Cataloging-in-Publication Data

Ernest Hemingway / edited and with an introduction by Harold Bloom.
p.   cm.—(Bloom's major short story writers)
Includes bibliographical references (p.) and index.
ISBN 0-7910-5121-8 (hc)
Hemingway, Ernest, 1899–1961 —Criticism and interpretation.
2. Short story.   I. Series.
PS3515.E37Z58654   1999
813'.52—dc21
98-42029
CIP

Chelsea House Publishers
1974 Sproul Road, Suite 400
Broomall, PA 19008-0914

Contributing Editor: Gwendolyn Bellerman

11/7/02 $22.95

Contents

User's Guide

This volume is designed to present biographical, critical, and bibliographical information on the author's best-known or most important short stories. Following Harold Bloom's editor's note and introduction is a detailed biography of the author, discussing major life events and important literary accomplishments. A plot summary of each short story follows, tracing significant themes, patterns, and motifs in the work, and an annotated list of characters supplies brief information on the main characters in each story.

A selection of critical extracts, derived from previously published material from leading critics, analyzes aspects of each short story. The extracts consist of statements from the author, if available, early reviews of the work, and later evaluations up to the present. A bibliography of the author's writings (including a complete list of all books written, cowritten, edited, and translated), a list of additional books and articles on the author and the work, and an index of themes and ideas in the author's writings conclude the volume.

~

Harold Bloom is Sterling Professor of the Humanities at Yale University and Henry W. and Albert A. Berg Professor of English at the New York University Graduate School. He is the author of over 20 books and the editor of more than 30 anthologies of literary criticism.

Professor Bloom's works include *Shelley's Mythmaking* (1959), *The Visionary Company* (1961), *Blake's Apocalypse* (1963), *Yeats* (1970), *A Map of Misreading* (1975), *Kabbalah and Criticism* (1975), and *Agon: Toward a Theory of Revisionism* (1982). *The Anxiety of Influence* (1973) sets forth Professor Bloom's provocative theory of the literary relationships between the great writers and their predecessors. His most recent books include *The American Religion* (1992), *The Western Canon* (1994), *Omens of Millennium: The Gnosis of Angels, Dreams, and Resurrection* (1996), and *Shakespeare: The Invention of the Human* (1998).

Professor Bloom earned his Ph.D. from Yale University in 1955 and has served on the Yale faculty since then. He is a 1985 MacArthur Foundation Award recipient and served as the Charles Eliot Norton Professor of Poetry at Harvard University in 1987–88. He is currently the editor of other Chelsea House series in literary criticism, including BLOOM'S NOTES, BLOOM'S MAJOR POETS, MAJOR LITERARY CHARACTERS, MODERN CRITICAL VIEWS, MODERN CRITICAL INTERPRETATIONS, and WOMEN WRITERS OF ENGLISH AND THEIR WORKS.

Editor's Note

My Introduction pays tribute to the style and quasi-Shake-spearean mode of characterization in the best of Ernest Hemingway's short stories.

The Critical Extracts are too copious and too varied to indicate more than a few high points here. These begin with Robert Penn Warren on "the gallantry of defeat" and Sean O'Faolin on what *he* calls Hemingway's philosophical shallowness. Robert Wooster Stallman explicates Harry's internal monologues in "Kilimanjaro," while Lionel Trilling shrewdly comments upon "Hills Like White Elephants."

Annette Benert dissents from most critics by finding "A Clean, Well-Lighted Place" to be affirmative rather than nihilistic, after which Steven Hoffman explores the same story's sense of dread. In a very original contribution, Doris Lanier subtly reveals the thematic significance of absinthe in "Hills Like White Elephants," while the feminist critic Nina Baym brilliantly comments upon Margot Macomber's dilemmas in "The Short, Happy Life of Francis Macomber."

Introduction

HAROLD BLOOM

Hemingway's sublimity is attained in the best of his short stories, and not in his novels. Even *The Sun Also Rises* is not of the eminence of the Nick Adams stories or the four great narratives examined in this volume. Though endlessly parodied, voluntarily and involuntarily, Hemingway's style in the major stories remains astonishingly fresh: it continues to make us see more clearly. This achievement has limits; Hemingway is not Shakespeare, who uniquely enables us to see what we never could have seen without him. But no one else is Shakespeare either, and Hemingway, a century after his birth, almost rivals Walt Whitman as an American original, the master of an American way of seeing and feeling. Though Hemingway asserted that Mark Twain was his American precursor, his true father was Whitman:

> This grass is very dark to be from the white heads of old mothers,
> Darker than the colorless beards of old men,
> Dark to come from under the faint red roofs of mouths.

The Whitman who could proclaim that: "Agonies are one of my changes of garments," and that: "I am the man; I suffered; I was there," broke the new road for Hemingway's style. Wallace Stevens and Robert Penn Warren each asserted that Hemingway essentially was a poet, and perhaps the shorter stories–"In Another Country," "Hills Like White Elephants," "A Clean, Well-Lighted Place"–should be read as extended lyrics, prose-poems of surpassing intensity. My own favorite among all of Hemingway's brief stories is the wonderfully rancid "God Rest You Merry, Gentlemen" where the mordant Doc Fischer prophesies Nathanael West's magnificent Shrike in *Miss Lonelyhearts*. A lucid nihilism, of Doc Fischer's kind, always severely qualifies Hemingway's nostalgia for the consolations of religion. That nihilism, grandly explicit in "A Clean, Well-Lighted Place" and "Hills Like White Elephants," touches apotheosis in the more elaborate and varied "The Short Happy Life of Francis Macomber" and in the visionary "The Snows of Kilimanjaro."

All four of these stories were among Hemingway's own favorites. Unlike the Nick Adams stories–which include such classics as "The Light of the World," "The Killers," "In Another Country," and "Big

Two-Hearted River"—the four stories analyzed here at least attempt *not* to center upon a Hemingway-surrogate, like Nick Adams. And yet "Kilimanjaro" barely detaches Hemingway from Harry, the dying and self-betrayed writer. Of Harry, Hemingway observes: "He had loved too much, demanded too much, and he wore it all out." That would be a very accurate description of Shakespeare's King Lear, who seems to have been Hemingway's favorite character in the plays. The nihilism (as I interpret it) of Shakespeare's high tragedies is too remorseless a standard to set for Hemingway (or for anyone else), but Hemingway never stopped learning from the dramatist described by Colonel Cantwell in *Across the River and Into the Trees* as "the winner and still the undisputed champion."

What is wonderfully Shakespearean about the characters in Hemingway's best short stories is that they join us in *overhearing* themselves. This imparts an authentic depth to the young woman in "Hills Like White Elephants," to the waiters in "A Clean, Well-Lighted Place," and to Francis Macomber and to Harry, two dying and yet newly reborn sensibilities. It is so dangerous—really fatal— to compare any author to Shakespeare that I make this point only very tentatively, and yet Hemingway, in certain moments, can sustain it. He had learned from Shakespeare (and not, as he thought, from Joseph Conrad), how to interfuse detachment and sympathy in regard to his protagonists. That interfusion, and the triumph of his style, combine to render the finest of Hemingway's stories a permanent achievement. ❀

Biography of Ernest Hemingway

(1899–1961)

Born on July 21, 1899, Ernest Hemingway grew up in the peaceful town of Oak Park, Illinois, a suburb of Chicago also known as the hometown of architect Frank Lloyd Wright. His father, Clarence Hemingway, was a physician who loved the outdoors and took Ernest on long camping and hunting trips in the north woods of Michigan. Here Hemingway developed his lifelong love of action and adventure, and these woodland experiences form the background for his vivid Nick Adams stories.

Hemingway distinguished himself in high school both as the editor of his high school newspaper and for his skill in boxing and football. While boxing Hemingway injured his eye so seriously that he could not, despite repeated attempts, enlist to fight in World War I. He moved to Kansas City immediately after graduation, lying about his age in order to be hired as a cub reporter on the *Kansas City Star*. Although he worked for the *Star* only for a year, he drank in the discipline of a newswriter. Use short sentences. Write with action words. Never use an adjective when a vivid verb will relay the event. Cut your words and cut them again.

Within a year of joining the *Star*, Hemingway joined a volunteer American Red Cross ambulance unit as a driver and went to the Italian front. He was seriously wounded at Fossalta on the Italian Piave on July 8, 1918, his body ripped by more than 200 steel splinters from an exploding mortar. Hemingway crawled out of his trench into an open-fire zone to rescue a wounded Italian soldier, only to be pinned down by a barrage of Austrian machine gun fire. Nonetheless, he managed to drag both himself and the wounded Italian to safety and was later awarded the Italian medal al Valore Militare. After multiple operations and recuperation in Milan, he joined the Italian infantry, an experience he developed later in *A Farewell to Arms*.

Discharged in 1919, Hemingway returned to journalism in a job as feature writer for the *Toronto Star* and crime reporter for the

Chicago Tribune. He soon thereafter met and married Hadley Richardson, with whom he moved to Paris as a foreign correspondent. Here he joined one of the most glamorous and stimulating gatherings of writers in Europe: the salon of Gertrude Stein. Gathered around Stein were authors including Ezra Pound and F. Scott Fitzgerald, the "lost generation" of writers who felt that the war had shattered their hopes, who saw the horrors of the battlefield as neither noble nor patriotic, but merely the detritus of greedy, materialistic governments.

In Paris Hadley became pregnant with Hemingway's first child, his son John. Also in Paris Hemingway suffered a horrible setback to his literary aspirations. On a train platform Hadley's suitcase was stolen. In it were Hemingway's first completed novel, 18 short stories, and 30 poems. Nonetheless, he recovered his notes and went on to publish his first collection, *Three Stories and Ten Poems*. It was published in France and received almost no notice. His next works, *In Our Time* and *The Torrents of Spring*, a satire of the American and Parisian literary scene, also sank without a trace, and it was not until the publication of *The Sun Also Rises* in 1926 that he received the critical and popular acclaim he enjoyed through most of his career. This novel, focusing on the heroic matador Pedro Romero and a group of American and British expatriates, introduced typical Hemingwayesque themes of love, honor, and draining disillusionment.

Between 1926 and 1940, Hemingway's restless passions led him to two divorces and several homes, among them his famous "mansion" in Key West and the lovely Finca Vigia in Cuba. His father's suicide in 1928, after long struggles with hypertension and diabetes, threw a shadow over Hemingway's life, and *A Farewell to Arms* echoes much of his own despair over the pointlessness of life in the face of the evils and stupidity of war and death. During this time he also traveled to Africa on safari, transforming his experiences into "The Snows of Kilimanjaro," "The Short, Happy Life of Francis Macomber," and *The Green Hills of Africa*.

Hemingway also watched in rage and horror as his beloved Spain was wracked by the civil war that erupted in 1936. Arriving at the front as a war correspondent, he soon became caught up in more active involvement. He raised $40,000 to buy ambulances for the Loyalists fighting for democracy against Franco's fascist troops and then joined the Loyalists themselves, blowing up bridges and capturing prisoners.

Hemingway was equally active in World War II as a correspondent with Patton's Third Army for *Collier's* magazine. In a famous episode, he took part in a skirmish during the liberation of Paris. Followed by a ragtag bunch of guerrilla soldiers, he "captured" the Ritz hotel, leaving a placard nailed to the front that read "Papa took good hotel. Plenty of good stuff in the cellar." In more serious moments he gathered intelligence on the movements of German forces and eventually was awarded the Bronze Star for bravery.

Despite the success of *For Whom the Bell Tolls* in 1940, Hemingway was haunted by fears that he was written out, that he had nothing more of importance to say. He anxieties were exacerbated by the publication of *Across the River and Into the Trees*, a light romance that is generally regarded as his weakest work. He rallied, however, in 1952 with *The Old Man and the Sea*, a novella that earned him the Pulitzer Prize in 1953 and a storm of praise.

In 1954 Hemingway was on an African safari with his fourth wife, Mary Welsh, a correspondent for *Time* magazine, when tragedy hit once again. Their plane crashed, causing serious internal and spinal injuries and leading to reports of their deaths. In a horrible coincidence, the plane that arrived to rescue them also crashed, leaving the couple terribly injured and far from help. However, Hemingway learned in his boxing career to "never stay down" and survived, soon returning to his brawling, hard-drinking life.

His greatest triumph awaited him in 1954, when he was awarded the Nobel Prize in Literature for *The Old Man and the Sea*, which the awards committee lauded for its "powerful style-forming mastery of the art of modern narration."

But even Hemingway's iron constitution could not withstand the years of fighting, war, long fishing and hunting trips, and mercurial passions. Retired to his beloved home in the mountains of Ketchum, Idaho, with his Mary and an endless parade of cats, Papa Hemingway was plagued by high blood pressure and depression. On the night of July 2, 1961, he could stand his weariness and weakness no longer and killed himself with a double-barreled shotgun.

Hemingway was both a swaggering adventurer and a skillful craftsman. He revised his work endlessly, laboring to catch the most subtle of emotions with his sparse, telegraphic language. He lived life as largely as he could, endlessly generous to friends yet quick to anger, exuberantly joyful yet shadowed by the ever-present fear of failure and death. His work is largely pessimistic, recognizing the spirit of *nada*, nothingness, that lurks behind the glories of fame and fate. Nonetheless, below this darkness lies a deep compassion, a sense of some ephemeral love and truth that can exist in the passing moment of human existence. He brought a new spirit of realism to American literature, a new ability to capture what really is and what makes us who we are. ❀

Plot Summary of
"A Clean, Well-Lighted Place"

"A Clean, Well-Lighted Place" is one of Hemingway's most deceiving stories. Only about five pages long, it has almost no overt action. The story consists almost entirely of dialogue and interior monologue. Yet in this subdued, quiet tale Hemingway creates a mood of profound grimness and futility, balanced by surprising tenderness and humanity. The plain nature of his style creates the powerful effect here, for the style mirrors his most essential point: Although courage can be won in the face of great excitement—on the battlefield, in the face of a charging lion, or on a towering mountaintop—it can also be won in the daily, personal struggle against existential despair. It is this simple battle for dignity and order that Hemingway portrays so starkly. In "The Art of the Short Story," an essay published in 1959, Hemingway said that he worked to "leave everything out" of "A Clean, Well-Lighted Place," and by leaving out everything extraneous he focuses the reader's attention on the elemental contest between darkness and light.

The story is simple. Two waiters sit in a pleasant Spanish café late at night, waiting for their last customer to leave. He, an old man, is reluctant to stop drinking his brandy and go back to his dark, lonely home. But it is late, and the younger waiter wants to return to his waiting wife. The two discuss the old man, mentioning his recent attempt at suicide. It is here that Hemingway quietly introduces the concept of *nada*—the Spanish word for nothing—while at the same time pointing out the terrible lack of insight that makes *nada* so frightening. One waiter asks why the old man tried to kill himself:

> "Why?"
> "He was in despair."
> "What about?"
> "Nothing."
> "How do you know it was nothing?"
> "He has plenty of money."

Although Hemingway is careful to not identify which speaker is which, most critics have seen the questioner as the old waiter. To the young waiter, nothing, *nada*, is unimportant, it is a lack of reason for death. Because the old man has money, he should be content. Yet to the old waiter nothing is clearly Something, and the despair of this

15

Something is a readily understandable cause for suicide. Throughout the story, the old man's suicide attempt is treated with great sympathy, which may relate to Hemingway's feelings about his own father's suicide in 1928.

As the waiters watch the old man, a young soldier walks by on the street with a woman on his arm. Their hurried passage through the light accentuates the darkness and emptiness of the night. The old man asks for another drink, and the young waiter complains that he will get home late to his waiting wife. He hurries back to his companion, and the two gossip about the old man. This dialogue is the most confusing part of the story. Hemingway does not differentiate who speaks what lines, and it seems that the older waiter is suddenly no longer in the know about the old man's situation. Some critics have argued that Hemingway simply became confused or forgetful, or that he chose purposely to give the older waiter a sort of ironic "ignorance." He already knows, but by allowing the younger waiter to chatter on he subtly points out the young man's inability to hear what he is told.

Finally the old man asks for another brandy and the young waiter refuses to serve him. "Finished," he says, "speaking with the omission of syntax stupid people employ when talking to drunken people or foreigners." He is stupid in the way of those who cannot see and cannot hear. The two waiters close down the café, with the younger man hurrying to get home. "We are of two different kinds," says the old man as they work. But the difference is not just that the young man has "everything," that is, "youth, confidence and a job," while the older waiter has only his work, but that the older man is reluctant to close the café and turn away those who need its comfort. He realizes that *bodegas* and bars, as opposed to the clean, well-lit café, do not provide the comfort and order that are so necessary. In fact, the crowded noise and darkness of a bar take away man's dignity as much as it restores his spirits.

As the older waiter walks home, he contemplates the terrible nothingness that is a man. "Our nada who art in nada, nada be thy name . . ." he thinks to himself, parodying the Lord's Prayer. "Hail nothing full of nothing, nothing is with thee," he thinks as he walks into a bar. Nowhere else in his fiction is Hemingway as clear about the connection between religion and despair. Although he himself converted to Catholicism and went regularly to Mass, here he strips away the comfort of faith and reduces it to meaningless symbols. Salvation is found not in outward show or words but in the small moments of grace and humanity in which one human being cares for another enough to provide light and cleanliness.

The waiter stops at a bar for a cup of coffee, then goes home to lie awake in his bed until dawn. "It is probably insomnia," he thinks, but the coming of the light and his ability to sleep are far more important than mere insomnia when set against the rest of the story.

Unlike "The Short, Happy Life of Francis Macomber" and Hemingway's more dramatic tales, "A Clean, Well-Lighted Place" emphasizes man's ability to endure rather than his ability to act. What is most devastating in this tale is emptiness, a loss of faith, a lack of spiritual underpinnings and external connections. As readers, we are filled with pity and with respect. Hemingway has turned his art like a magnifying glass upon a brief moment when nothing seems to happen, and has shown us the private battles going on every moment and resulting in a quiet heroism. He has indeed "left everything out," but he has also captured a world within a moment.

"A Clean, Well-Lighted Place" has often been compared to T. S. Eliot's "The Wasteland" in its discussion of spiritual loss. The concept of *nada* is more fully developed here than in any of Hemingway's other works. In this story *nada* is the metaphysical darkness of chaos, loneliness, and abandonment that lurks behind everything that makes life meaningful. In the face of *nada*, man is alone in an alien world, a place where faith and belief have become words repeated by rote to no effect. The older waiter is fully aware of the power of this darkness: "What did he fear? It was not fear or dread. It was a nothing that he knew too well. It was all a nothing and man was a nothing too." Ranged against this nihilistic despair are the forces of light and order represented by the café. There all is clean and peaceful, with a gentle companionship that fends off the night. This sense of order, though, is artificial and fleeting, and lasts only until the haste and selfishness of the young waiter causes the café to close for the night. In the end, everyone must face the darkness alone, some with dignity and some without. ❀

List of Characters in
"A Clean, Well-Lighted Place"

The *young waiter* would seem to be the antithesis of *nada*. He has youth, confidence, and a wife and home to return to. Yet he is the one most lacking in "light," the insight that gives the older waiter so much of his sympathy and ultimate heroism. The young waiter's callow ignorance and lack of sympathy make it impossible that he will ever recognize, let alone cope with, the profound despair of nothingness that surrounds him. He is blind to both what he has and what he lacks. His hurry to close the café illustrates his self-centered concern for his own life, while his clipped speech to the old man reveals his stupidity. For Hemingway, heroism consists at least in part in the ability to comprehend the void and then face it; the young waiter's bovine indifference renders him incapable of any such human insight or courage.

The *old, deaf man,* sitting in the shadows of the trees at the café, is an allegorical figure of despair. He comes to the café for solace, yet even in the depths of his brandy glass can do no more than hold off the darkness for a brief moment. Recently he tried to commit suicide by hanging himself but was cut down by his niece. In the death of his wife and his own attempted suicide he has faced the darkness of *nada*, yet he has no spiritual defenses against it. The old man is the figure of the one who had everything; he is wealthy and was presumably happily married until his wife died some time ago. He is clean and dignified, yet he is utterly alone and comfortless. Through his despair, his pitiful need to stay alone and neglected at the café, Hemingway provides a window into the ephemeral nature of human happiness.

Caught between the other two figures in terms of age, the *middle-aged waiter* spiritually rises above them both with his dignified, stoic courage in the face of the terrible chaos of nothingness. In contrast to the younger waiter, he would seem to have nothing in his life. He lives alone, with only his work to sustain him, and is plagued by insomnia. Yet it is his ability to care for and empathize with the old man that gives this story its sensitivity and pathos. The older waiter is alive to the potential of those around him, alive to their needs and their pasts, and is willing to sacrifice himself for their comfort. He is the keeper of the essential light and cleanliness at the café, and he tries gently to teach the young waiter about the realities of existence. At the end of the story, the bartender asks him, "What's yours?" the old waiter replies "Nada." However, in reality he has all of the compassion, strength, and dignity of Hemingway's most powerful heroes. ❀

Critical Views on
"A Clean, Well-Lighted Place"

ROBERT PENN WARREN ON VIOLENCE AND
MEANINGLESSNESS

[A three-time Pulitzer Prize winner, Robert Penn Warren
(1905–1989) became the first Poet Laureate of the United
States in 1986. Along with Cleanth Brooks, he co-edited the
Southern Review and wrote several volumes of criticism.
Brooks and Robert Penn Warren are known as two of the
founders of New Criticism, which looks at literature as a pure
art form, removed from the biographical and historical background of the author and era. He taught for many years at
Yale and Louisiana State University. Robert Penn Warren was
the author of *All the King's Men*, a fictional account of gov-
ernor Huey Long, *Band of Angels*, a novel, *Segregation: The
Inner Conflict of the South,* and many other works. In this
selection he discusses how violence and meaninglessness, or
nada, work together in Hemingway's fiction.]

And the sleepless man—the man obsessed by death, by the meaninglessness of the world, by nothingness, by nada—is one of the recurring symbols in the works of Hemingway. In this phase Hemingway
is a religious writer. The despair beyond plenty of money, the despair
which makes a sleeplessness beyond insomnia, is the despair felt by a
man who hungers for the certainties and meaningfulness of a religious faith but who cannot find in his world a ground for that faith.

Another recurring symbol, we have said, is the violent man. But
the sleepless man and the violent man are not contradictory but
complementary symbols. They represent phases of the same question, the same hungering for meaning in the world. The sleepless
man is the man brooding upon nada, upon chaos, upon Nature-as-
all. (For Nature-as-all equals moral chaos; even its bulls and lions
and kudu are not admired by Hemingway as creatures of conscious
self-discipline; their courage is meaningful only in so far as it symbolizes human courage.) The violent man is the man taking an
action appropriate to the realization of the fact of nada. He is, in

other words, engaged in the effort to discover human values in a naturalistic world. . . .

The violence, although in its first aspect it represents a sinking into nature, at the same time, in its second aspect, represents a conquest of nature, and of nada in man. It represents such a conquest, not because of the fact of violence, but because the violence appears in terms of discipline, a style, and a code. It is, as we have already seen, in terms of a self-imposed discipline that the heroes make one gallant, though limited, effort to redeem the incoherence of the world: they attempt to impose some form upon the disorder of their lives, the technique of the bull fighter or sportsman, the discipline of the soldier, the fidelity of the lover, or even the code of the gangster, which, though brutal and apparently dehumanizing, has its own ethic.

The discipline, the form, is never quite capable of subduing the world, but fidelity to it is part of the gallantry of defeat. By fidelity to it the hero manages to keep one small place "clean" and "well-lighted," and manages to retain, or achieve for one last moment, his dignity. As the old Spanish waiter muses, there should be a "clean, well-lighted place" where one could keep one's dignity at the late hour.

—Robert Penn Warren, "Hemingway," *The Kenyon Review* 11, No. 1 (Winter 1947): 1–28

WARREN BACHE COMPARES WAITERS IN "A CLEAN, WELL-LIGHTED PLACE"

[Warren Bache has written many articles on William Faulkner as well as a critical study of William Shakespeare, entitled *Measure for Measure as Dialectical Art: Shakespeare's Deliberate Art.* In this extract he compares the young waiter to the old waiter, reading the short story not as a "conflict of youth with age" but as an investigation of how much the two are really alike.]

In Hemingway's fiction, "the interest in conduct and the attitude toward conduct is central." To express this focus on conduct in "A Clean, Well-Lighted Place" Hemingway seems to have represented—

his fiction, rather than being a report, is always a suggestive, dramatic representation—two ways of life: the young waiter standing for a materialistic way of life; the older waiter and the old man standing for a nihilistic (notice the parody of the Lord's Prayer) way of life. These two ways of life, since both are devoid of spiritual values, lead us to an awareness of the theme of the story: the dilemma of contemporary man living in a world of spiritual emptiness. The clean, well-lighted place is a symbolic substitute for the spiritual life. It is clean and orderly and well lighted, but it is only a substitute, and as such it is sterile. It signifies a nothingness, but a known and tangible and dignified nothingness; it is opposed to the intangible blackness and the unknown. The clean, well-lighted place is, like materialism, an opiate of the spirit.

Since the older waiter and the old man have much in common, it can be said that there is really only one conflict in the story: the conflict between the young man and the two older men. In a sense, then, this is the conflict of youth with age. The young waiter represents materialism because youth is not rarely materialistic, though with the passage of time materialism often loses its meaning, But reading the story with care, one discovers that the young waiter is even now clutching at the straws of materialism. There are numerous suggestions that the young waiter is aware, perhaps not intellectually but certainly emotionally, of the pitfalls and insecurities of a life based solely on materialism: the young waiter admits that there is a difference between drinking at home and drinking at the café; the young waiter takes offense at his fellow waiter's mild joke about his wife, although a few lines later he is to assert that he is all confidence; in brief, throughout the story the young waiter seems to be protesting too much. From all this we can assume that the two waiters are not of two different kinds as the older waiter says; rather, the young waiter's attitude toward life is more akin to the older waiter's than he would care to admit.

—Warren B. Bache, "Craftsmanship in 'A Clean, Well-Lighted Place,'" *The Personalist* 37, No. 1 (Winter 1956): 60–64

Sean O'Faolain on Realism and Kindness in "A Clean, Well-Lighted Place"

[Sean O'Faolain (1900–1991) was a celebrated Irish novelist, critic, and short story writer. He was extremely active in the Irish independence movement, working as the publicity director for the Irish Republican Army, and his fictional works evoke a strong and abiding love for his country and its heritage. His works include *The Talking Tree and Other Stories, Bird Alone, The Story of Ireland, Come Back to Erin,* and an autobiography, *Vive Moi!.* In this excerpt he discusses the interplay between realism and kindness in one of Hemingway's most cryptic and seemingly nihilistic stories.]

Here is a story, if there ever was one, with what are called "unsuspected depths." A reader might, in a tired moment, go through it casually, unaffected, or at any rate not much affected, and if asked afterwards what it was all about have some trouble in giving a meaningful answer. No reader whose sensibilities were awake could fail to be aware that he was being unusually stirred, yet even he also might have difficulty in saying what it is all about. It is something of a joke, in view of the common belief that Hemingway is a tough, laconic writer, that the reason for the difficulty is that this story by an acknowledged "realist" is as near, in its quality and its effect, to a poem as prose can be without ceasing to be honest prose. I put the word "realist" in quotation marks because these stock terms prove to be inadequate whenever we apply to literature the primal test, not what it is meaning, or saying, but of what it is doing to us—what kind of emotional satisfaction, or pleasure, it is giving us, of what quality, at what level. That is the primal test; afterward it is our secondary pleasure to "see how well he did it."

Our feelings here are, surely, mainly of pity and awe. We spend a bit of a night—by inference, many, many nights, by extension a whole life—in the company of three Spaniards, one very old, one middle-aged, one still young. The camera is angled, at a distance, on a café-front; it closes in on an old man, who says only two words; it passes from him to the two waiters; it ends with the middle-aged waiter, and it rests longest on him. With him it becomes a ray entering into his soul. Age, death, despair, love, the boredom of life, two elderly men seeking sleep and forgetfulness, and one still young enough to feel passion, cast into an hour and a place whose silence and emptiness, soon to become more silent and more empty still—it all creates in us, at first, a sad mood in which patience and futility feebly strive with one another, involve us, mesmerize us. Grimness is in the offing. Hemingway's kindness and tenderness save us from that. For Hemingway, deep down, is one of the kindest and most tender of writers. If our final feelings here are of pity and awe it is he who communicates them to us. I believe that Hemingway's "realism" is merely the carapace or shell that protects, grips, holds from over-spilling a nature fundamentally emotional and tender.

—Sean O'Faolain, "A Clean, Well-Lighted Place," *Hemingway: A Collection of Critical Essays*, ed. Robert P. Weeks (Englewood Cliffs, NJ: Prentice-Hall, 1962): 112–113

JACKSON J. BENSON ON IRONY IN "A CLEAN, WELL-LIGHTED PLACE"

[Jackson J. Benson is a well-known critic of modern American fiction. He has published *The True Adventures of John Steinbeck, Writer: A Biography,* and *Looking for Steinbeck's Ghost,* and edited works on Steinbeck, Hemingway, and Bernard Malamud. He is a professor of comparative literature and English at San Diego State University. In this selection he discusses the ironic paradoxes and puns of "A Clean, Well-Lighted Place."]

Many recent discussions of this story emphasize Hemingway's presentation of "nothingness" as a real entity, a presentation which appears to involve a strikingly profound intuitive proposal by a writer who has been thought to be so unphilosophic in his orientation to life. Commented on less, but equally important to the theme of the story, is the emphasis placed on the awareness of the older waiter. In looking back over the story, the reader should note how much of the story is devoted to the older waiter's clear and accurate perceptions of himself, of the other two characters, and of what might generally be termed "the situation." The fundamental irony of the story lies in the skillfully balanced and controlled contrast between the attitude of boredom (self-absorption) displayed by the young waiter, who has "everything," and the active concern and essential "aliveness" of the older waiter, who has "nothing." The ironic paradox that results is that only through the awareness of nothing or non-meaning can meaning be created. At a certain point in one's experience with this story, paradoxes and puns begin to trip over themselves. Like Miss Van Campen in *A Farewell to Arms*, the younger waiter is in a service occupation; it is his profession to think of others, but he neither serves nor waits. Whether it was in Hemingway's mind or not, I cannot help adding that the younger waiter has not yet learned (to quote from Milton's "*blindness* sonnet," which talks of Milton's relation to God's scheme and begins "When I consider how my *light* is spent"): "They also serve who only stand and wait."

Blindness versus awareness is Hemingway's most pervasive theme, and it is borne on a rippling wave of irony into almost everything he writes. Seeing oneself, others, and the situation clearly is the basic requirement for the creation of meaning—genuine concern or love for others. Illusion and self-centeredness are the enemies of meaning, just as the younger waiter is hostile to the old man and impatient with the older waiter.

—Jackson J. Benson, *Hemingway: The Writer's Art of Self-Defense* (Minneapolis: University of Minnesota Press, 1969): 117–118

❧

WARREN BENNETT ON THE SOLDIER AND HIS GIRL IN "A CLEAN, WELL-LIGHTED PLACE"

[A noted scholar on Ernest Hemingway, Warren Bennett has contributed to *Hemingway Review* and other journals. He teaches English at the University of Regina in Canada. In this excerpt he discusses how the appearance of the soldier and his girl in "A Clean, Well-Lighted Place" serves to accentuate the loneliness of this tale and cast the young waiter into the role of tragic hero.]

In the silence that takes place immediately following the older waiter's ironic "'He has plenty of money,'" a girl and a soldier went by in the street. The street light shone on the brass number on his collar. The girl wore no head covering and hurried beside him.

> Y.W. "The guard will pick him up," one waiter said.
> O.W. "What does it matter if he gets what he's after?"
> Y.W. "He had better get off the street now. The guard will get him. They went by five minutes ago."

The younger waiter emphasizes the military guards because to him they represent guardians of a culture in which one may be confident of success. He is not concerned about the soldier. Individual needs, whether they are the need of a girl or the need to drink for a lonely old man, must be sacrificed to the punctuality of the job, the ignorant securities of rule and routine. The younger waiter wants everyone off the street, as he wants the old man out of the café. He wants to be off the streets himself, and is, in effect, also a kind of guard. "'No more tonight. Close now,'" he says to the old man and begins "pulling down the metal shutters."

But the older waiter does understand that agonizing lack of an individual: "'What does it matter if he gets what he's after. Company punishment will be minor compared to the anguish of being alone. Everything is a temporary stay against despair, light for the night, another drink, relations with a girl. "'You can't tell,'" even the old man "'might be better with a wife.'"

The soldier's kinship with the older waiter and the old man is illustrated by the metaphor of light and something clean or polished: "The street light shone on the brass number on his collar." They are all of a "kind," the soldier as disillusioned with the military machine as the older waiter and the old man are disillusioned with the machine of the world. The soldier is not concerned about cunning as the old man is not concerned about letting the café close. The soldier needs the sexual intoxication of this girl as the older waiter and the old man need a drink. The soldier is no more concerned about military regulations than the old man is concerned about financial regulations, and "would leave without paying" if he became too drunk. "As Hemingway once put it, 'There is honor among pickpockets and honor among whores. It is simply that the standards differ.'"

The scene—a prostitute and a soldier—is the epitome of a meaningless and chaotic world full of loopholes: an interwoven fabric of ironies punctured by nothingness. Everything is possible through love or aggression, but paradoxically nothing is permanent. There is a constant, desperate struggle against the coefficients of adversity. Living becomes a deadly affair, or conflict, essentially devoid of humor because everything is ultimately a "dirty trick."

This is the basis for the older waiter's not so funny "joke" later in the story. The younger waiter has just suggested that the old man could buy a bottle and drink at home, to which the older waiter replies, " 'It's not the same.' "

> "No, it is not," agreed the waiter with a wife. He did not wish to be unjust. He was only in a hurry.
> "And you? You have no fear of going home before your usual hour?"
> "Are you trying to insult me?"
> "No, hombre, only to make a joke."
> "No," the waiter who was in a hurry said...
> "I have confidence. I am all confidence."

The joke is crucial and hinges directly on the scene with the girl and the soldier. Structurally and texturally they establish the love wound motif which is so dominant in Hemingway that it becomes the other side of the same psychic coin as the war wound. Through either the death of one of the partners or the inability of one partner to fulfill the promise of love—satisfy the other's needs—an individual is isolated and pushed to despair by the failure of the love alliance.

The complete working out of this motif is the "real end" which Hemingway omitted, and the phrase "waiter with a wife" preceding the joke, functions as a lens to bring into focus the catastrophe which the younger waiter will face. When the younger waiter goes home before his "usual time," his wife will be gone, or perhaps, though at home in bed, engaged in another desperate relationship. The girl and the soldier appear again like ghosts, only this time the girl without a "head covering," ironically "hurrying," is suggestive of the younger waiter's wife.

The story now becomes superbly charged with dramatic as well as verbal irony. The younger waiter's confidence dissolves into tragic hubris, and his statements, such as "'I'm not lonely,'" are imbued with an impending doom that is near classic. Situations become ironically transferred. The old man's despair and loneliness without a wife, the older waiter's insomnia and need of light, the soldier's risk for temporary sexual meaning—all are now the younger waiter's future. At the very moment that he is playing the heartless and uncompromising judge, he is also reality's dupe and victim. Whatever he has said about the others may soon be said about him. And with equal irony, he has "hurried" to his own undoing. His all-confident intentions will be reversed. His recognition of another truth is imminent. The radical contingencies of life will have taught him the absurdity of the human condition, and the twist of events will topple him from his pinnacle of confidence into the phantasmagoria where the older waiter and the old man cling despairingly to their clean, well-lighted place. The younger waiter will become a new member of Hemingway's collection: *Winner Take Nothing.*

—Warren Bennett, "Character, Irony and Resolution in 'A Clean, Well-Lighted Place,'" *American Literature* 42, No. 1 (March 1970): 70–79

（🌿）

ANNETTE BENERT ON HUMAN POTENTIAL IN "A CLEAN, WELL-LIGHTED PLACE"

[A professor of humanities at Allentown College of St. Francis DeSales, Annette Benert has written several articles on Edith Wharton, Henry James, and other authors. In this excerpt she analyzes "'A Clean, Well-Lighted Place." She does not see it as dark and nihilistic, as other critics have, but rather an affirmation of human potential in the face of despair.]

Perhaps belatedly, but at least on the evidence of imagery and characterization, we may now discuss the theme of the story. Most readers take the latter to be *nada*, making "A Clean, Well-Lighted Place," despite the title, a story about Nothingness and the pessimism and despair of the human response to it. This view ignores both the definition of nada inferable from the story and the nature of the old writer's response to it.

Despite Hemingway's manipulation of the pronoun *it*, the reader must not confuse Nothingness with the responses it produces, nor the response of the older waiter with that of the old man. *Nada* is depicted primarily spatially, as an objective reality, out there beyond the light; it is a final hard fact of human existence, though "some lived in it and never felt it," e.g., the younger waiter. In addition, it becomes temporal with the older waiter's repetition of "*y pues nada*" before the prayer. Though Carlos Baker, with great sensitivity, calls it "a Something called Nothing which is so huge, terrible, overbearing, inevitable, and omnipresent that, once experienced it can never be forgotten," which "bulks like a Jungian Shadow," its mythic qualities are perhaps not even that well defined.

More important, the response of the old patron—the search for oblivion through drunkenness or suicide—is not the only one, and certainly not the one of the older waiter. John Killinger observes that "the only entity truly capable of defying the encroachments of Nothingness is the individual," and Cleanth Brooks that "the order and the light are supplied by *him*," the old waiter, the individual. Carrying this affirmation one step further, Wayne Booth notes "a mood of bitterness against darkness combined with a determination to fight the darkness with light—if only the clean, well-lighted place of art itself." But, as we have seen, all the positive imagery, including light, is ironically undercut by the presence of a shadow side, and the "darkness" is counteracted on more levels than that simply of "light."

The older waiter in fact acts in various ways against Nothingness. He expresses solidarity with the old patron, and would willingly keep the café open as long as anyone wants it; he is instrumental in keeping the lights on. But his acquaintance with *nada* is intimate enough to keep him awake all night, every night; yet this hyper-awareness leads him neither toward self-destruction nor toward ego-centricity. He can fuse religious sensibility with existential anxiety into a parodic prayer, after which he can smile. Turning off the light in the café and going home to bed is a daily act of courage done silently, without complaint. His sensitivity to places which make dignity possible gives us the verbal clue that his life is one of survival with dignity.

Thematically, then, the older waiter actively demonstrates that life against *nada* is achieved by awareness, sensitivity, human solidarity, ritual (verbal and physical), humor, and courage. Together these qualities make dignity, or, to use Jamesian terms, style or form; we encounter them also in the good bullfighters in *Death in the Afternoon*, which may amplify the [theme] of that book as well as aesthetic relevance. Such attributes also lead to a double vision and a mode of expression which may be called irony, a potent antidote to both despair and pride. The older waiter, against the heaviest odds, is a man in control.

"A Clean, Well-Lighted Place" is, without cheating, a totally affirmative story, one of the very few in our literature. It assumes a world without meaning, life on the edge of the abyss, but that is not what it is about. It assumes a protagonist of acute awareness and minor characters of lesser consciousness, but it is not about that difference. It is, rather, a dramatization of the possibility, given the above conditions, of man continuing to act, to feel even for others, to think even about metaphysics, to create (with a smile), to control and thereby to humanize both himself and his environment. The older waiter is neither a hero nor a saint, but, to borrow from Camus, that more ambitious being, a man.

—Annette Benert, "Survival Through Irony: Hemingway's 'A Clean, Well-Lighted Place,'" Studies in Short Fiction 11, No. 2 (Spring 1974): 181–188

☙

STEVEN HOFFMAN ON "NADA" IN "A CLEAN, WELL-LIGHTED PLACE"

[Now a lawyer in Washington, D.C., Steven Hoffman taught English for many years at Virginia Polytechnic Institute and State University. He is a scholar of Emily Dickinson, Robert Lowell, Shirley Jackson, and other American authors. In this excerpt he discusses the theological and philosophical implications of "nada" in Hemingway's short story.]

In his crucial meditation at the end the old waiter makes it quite clear that *nada* is not an individual state but one with grave universal implication: "It was a nothing that he knew too well. It was *all* a nothing and a man was nothing too" [my italics]. According to William Barret, the *nada*-shadowed realm of "A Clean, Well-Lighted Place" is no less than a microcosm of the existential universe as defined by Martin Heidegger and the existentialist philosophers who came before and after him, principally Kierkegaard and Sartre. Barrett's position finds internal support in the old waiter's celebrated parody prayer: "Our nada who are in nada, nada be thy name thy kingdom nada thy will be nada in nada as it is in nada. Give us this nada our daily nada and nada us our nada as we nada our nadas and nada us not into nada but deliver us from nada; pues nada." The character's deft substitution of the word *nada* for all the key nouns (entities) and verbs (actions) in the Paternoster suggests the concept's truly metaphysical stature. Obviously, *nada* is to connote a series of significant absences: the lack of external physical or spiritual sustenance; the total lack of moral justification for action (in the broadest perspective, the essential meaninglessness of *any* action); and finally, the impossibility of deliverance from this situation.

The impact of *nada*, however, extends beyond its theological implications. Rather, in the Heideggerian sense ("das Nicht"), it is an umbrella term that subsumes all of the irrational, unforeseeable, existential forces that tend to infringe upon the human self, to make a "nothing." It is the absolute power of chance and circumstance to negate individual free will and the entropic tendency toward ontological disorder that perpetually looms over man's tenuous personal sense of order. But the most fearsome face of *nada*, and clear proof of man's radical contingency, is death—present here in the old man's wife's death and his own attempted suicide. Understandably, the old waiter's emotional response to this composite threat is mixed. It "was not fear or dread," which would imply a specific object to be feared, but a pervasive uneasiness, an existential anxiety that, according to Heidegger, arises when one becomes fully aware of the precarious status of his very being.

—Steven K. Hoffman, "Nada and the Clean, Well-Lighted Place: The Unity of Hemingway's Short Fiction, *Essays in Literature* 6, No. 1 (Spring 1979): 91–110

Plot Summary of
"Hills Like White Elephants"

Like "A Clean, Well-Lighted Place," "Hills Like White Elephants" is deceptive in its simplicity. Very little seems to take place: a couple sits at a train station in a small town in Spain, waiting for the train to Madrid. They talk and drink, and the story ends before the train even arrives. Yet within this quiet scene is a moral struggle, an investigation of the spiritual barrenness of modern love, that is piercing in its precision. The unspoken reason for their trip to Madrid, an abortion, hovers between them, poisoning every word. Hemingway does not cast moral judgment on the operation itself but on the narcissistic selfishness of the man, his inability to hear the young woman's unvoiced plea for home and a family. Her surrender at the end is no less poignant than the death of a soldier on the battlefield, both because of its inevitability and the powerlessness of her morality and desire in the face of his more modern egotism.

The story opens as the man and the woman sit in the shade of the station café, discussing what to drink to cool them down from the oppressive heat. The young woman looks across the valley at the dry, desolate hills, commenting that in the shimmer of hot air they look like white elephants. The white elephant has long been a symbol of a thing that has become useless and burdensome and is an apt metaphor for their relationship. The man refuses to acknowledge her imaginative view, though, and an argument sparks between them. She changes the subject, asking about the words painted on the bead curtain of the café. It is the name of a drink, Anis del Toro, and after tasting it she says its licorice taste reminds her of absinthe. "Everything tastes of licorice. Especially all the things you've waited so long for, like absinthe." "Oh, cut it out," he says, and again it is unclear why they are quarreling. Only when the reader realizes that she is remarking obliquely that everything she has longed for seems the same, in that it is ruined, does the emotional intensity of the scene make sense.

Absinthe is a particularly appropriate metaphor for other reasons as well. Long banned in the United States, France, and other countries because it is believed to cause madness and sterility, absinthe contains the poisonous hallucinogen wormwood. Because of its potency, it has also been seen as an aphrodisiac. The mention here thus hints at the connection between passion and barrenness in their relationship. She comments that "that's all we do, isn't it—look at things and try new drinks," pointing out how purposeless their life is as they drift from hotel to hotel across the dusty plains of Europe.

After another drink, the man begins to pressure the young woman on the subject of the abortion. "It's really an awfully simple operation . . . it's not really an operation at all . . . it's not really anything." By refusing to call it by its name, he believes he will make it less important, less real. But to her it is something awful, and she refuses to respond. She asks him what their relationship will be like afterward, and he assures her that all will be well. In his mind the pregnancy is the only thing that has made them unhappy, whereas she clearly sees not the pregnancy, but his reaction to it, as problematic. She comments, with bitter irony, that everyone she has known who has had an abortion has been "so happy," and he is stung by her misery. He claims that if she does not want to go through with it she does not need to, that he loves her so much that he is worried about her. But she believes him no more than does the reader.

She gets up and looks out over the valley. On the other side are the fertile fields along the river, with green trees and waving grain. She says, "And we could have had all this . . . And we could have had everything and every day we make it more impossible." To her the blooming fecundity of the fields is like her pregnancy, the everything of life that she so desperately wants. But he has not even been listening to her words, let alone their deeper meaning. "What did you say?" he asks, deaf to her emotional storm. She sits back down at the table, and now her eyes are fixed again on the dry hills on which nothing grows.

He tells her again that he does not want her to have the operation if it, or presumably the unborn child, "means anything to her." But his concern is undermined by his comment that he does not want anyone other than her, that his desire for her would be affected by the child. Pressed to her breaking point, she begs him to stop talking, and they sit in silence.

The waitress comes to tell them that the train will be arriving in five minutes, and the man offers to take their bags to the other side of the station. The compression of time in this story, the sense that the couple's moral existence is bounded by the inexorable timetable of the railway, adds to the powerful effect by concentrating the reader's attention.

The man takes the bags, and then stops by the bar. He drinks an Anis del Toro in ironic balance with the earlier scene in the story in which he had the same drink with the girl. Already he has begun to leave her, and the repetition of the drink emphasizes the sameness of his life whether she is with him or not. He returns to pick her up, and she assures him with a smile that "there's nothing wrong with me. I feel fine." Left with nothing, she has retreated into the brittle courtesy that is her only defense.

"Hills Like White Elephants" is a quiet but powerful commentary on the death of love, as traditional morality is eclipsed. By setting his tale in Spain, a Catholic country in which abortion would be especially horrific, Hemingway accentuates how alienated his characters are from their world, as well as from each other. Their communication is futile; he cannot see the white elephants, and she cannot see abortion as an "awfully simple operation." In this story, Hemingway's concise language leads each word, each fragment of dialogue, to resonate with meaning specifically because he does not create a definition for the reader. Yet the subtle and dramatic dialogue intimates the empty, shattered future and the despairing nothing that await the couple perfectly. In this story, selfishness is as destructive as the dark, nihilistic despair of the old man in "A Clean, Well-Lighted Place." ❈

List of Characters in
"Hills Like White Elephants"

A rootless, hedonistic American, *the man* is notable as much for his selfishness as his insensitivity. He refuses to respond to the girl's imaginative sallies about the hills being like white elephants and ignores her unspoken pleas for love and a family. His claims to love her and wish to do anything for her clearly are false, as he bullies her conversationally and refuses to accept responsibility for his actions. Although he sees himself as the voice of reason, caring only for facts and proof, he is blind to the results that the abortion will have upon the woman. He cannot see the truth of their barren existence. The American does not love her, and he is appalled at the notion of making a family with her.

Far more imaginative and emotional than her companion, the *young woman* is also much more vulnerable. She is isolated from those around her because she cannot speak Spanish, and she is quite aware that no matter what she does her relationship to the man has been shattered beyond recovery. Hemingway refers to her primarily as the "girl," rather than the "woman" to emphasize her powerlessness. The American calls her "Jig," a nickname that again accentuates her youth as well as the casual sexual nature of their relationship. She desperately wants to keep the child but is unable to succeed in any of her subtle, unspoken battles to win the man over to her needs and desires. In the end she realizes that her fantasies are as barren as the hills themselves. ✸

Critical Views on
"Hills Like White Elephants"

RICHARD W. LID ON THE NEED FOR SPEECH IN "HILLS
LIKE WHITE ELEPHANTS"

[A professor of English at California State University at
Northridge, Richard W. Lid is the author of *Ford Madox
Ford: The Essence of His Art* as well as numerous articles on
F. Scott Fitzgerald. In this excerpt he discusses the terrible
pressure to speak that afflicts Hemingway's characters in
"Hills Like White Elephants." Although talking can only
exacerbate their pain, the characters must nonetheless
express themselves.]

In Hemingway to speak is to lose something. The meaning of an
experience will disappear, as it did in "Soldier's Home" for Krebs,
who "acquired the nausea in regard to experience that is the result of
untruth or exaggeration." Indeed, to speak is often to invite further
pain; yet so great is the need for speech that Hemingway's characters
almost always make such a struggle, and it is these verbal actions
which occupy the foreground of many of his greatest stories.

Two stories by Hemingway, "Old Man at the Bridge" and "Hills
Like White Elephants," illustrate the extremes of such struggles in
Hemingway. The first story, a little incident of terror enacted against
a panorama of terror, revolves around a simple, almost inarticulate
old man who can barely find any words at all to express the feelings
which accompany his mute drama of life-and-death. The second
story, the author's favorite, deals with the socially taboo topic of
abortion and presents two highly sophisticated and articulate
people, unmarried lovers, now faced with the consequence of their
love and unable to communicate because their private language of
love has become unbearable. In each story the barrier to articulation
is the cost of being precise in language. To say truly what is felt is to
undergo more pain than it is possible to endure. The struggle for
words is painful. And yet, no matter the cost, speech is also the only
possible relief from pain—even if, as becomes apparent, the result
of speaking must mean more pain. Thus the old man gropes for
words to express his plight and can only reach anguish. Thus the

young couple hurt each other more and more as they obliquely talk around the abortion the mans wants the girl to have.

For the man and the girl such language is both a shield and a weapon. Under its aegis they are able to give vent to emotions too painful to face directly. Neither is enjoying the struggle of wills going on between them; both would keep it submerged as long as possible. Yet each has the need to express his feelings, and thus they both attack the relationship which has caused their predicament. The savor has gone from their intimacy; it is all a dreary sameness, like the inevitable taste of licorice in all the drinks they try. "That's the way with everything," the man says. In effect he is saying, "what did you expect? It was foolish to think that there would be anything unusual about our experience." In sum, the man has baldly reduced their private intimacy to the level of all such illicit affairs. "'Yes,' you've waited so long for, like absinthe.'" She is registering her disappointment in the romantic illusion. But absinthe is also a forbidden drink, banned by society because it can produce blindness. And illicit romance is similarly forbidden fruit, unlawful pleasure made more appealing by society's taboo. It too produces blindness—of a moral order; and the consequence of that blindness is what they now have to face. It is the romantic experience itself that the girl is now bitterly denying, for what did their intimacy, reduced to its essence, consist of but looking at things and talking about them in a private way and trying new drinks, acts which they can now only perform in an empty ritual of self-mockery. Indeed, as they talk their affair becomes more and more devoid of meaning, until, at the end of the story, it is completely leveled when the man's eyes fall on their bags, "labels on them from all the hotels where they had spent nights."

—Richard W. Lid, "Hemingway and the Need for Speech," *Modern Fiction Studies* 8, No. 4 (Winter 1962–1963): 401–407

[A brilliant critic and teacher, Lionel Trilling (1905–1975) is
known for his ability to bring enormous clarity to the literature he discusses. He taught at Columbia University, Harvard, and Oxford, and counted Allen Ginsberg and John
Hollander among his students. He is the author of *Mind in
the Modern World, Beyond Culture: Essays on Literature and
Learning, The Literal Imagination: Essays on Literature and
Society*, and other works. In this selection, taken from his
book *The Experience of Literature: A Reader with Commentaries*, Trilling explores Hemingway's use of imagination
and reason in "Hills Like White Elephants."]

Should we need a clue to where the point of the story lies, we can
find it in a single word in the last of the few brief passages of narration, the paragraph which tells us that the man carries the bags to
the other side of the station. "Coming back, he walked through the
barroom, where people waiting for the train were drinking. He
drank an Anis at the bar and looked at the people. They were all
waiting reasonably for the train." Waiting *reasonably*—it is a strange
adverb for the man's mind to have lighted on. (We might note that
by his use of this word, Hemingway does, for an instant, betray a
knowledge of the man's internal life.) Why not *quietly*, or *apatheti-
cally*, or *stolidly*? Why should he choose to remark upon the people's
reasonableness, taking note of it with approval, and as if it made a
bond of community between him and them? It is because he, a reasonable man, has been having a rough time reasoning with an
unreasonable woman.

Nor do we need the girl's tones of voice labelled for us. We understand that she is referring to a desire which she does not know how
to defend in words and that therefore she speaks in bitterness and
irony. She wants to have the child. There is no possible way to for-
mulate a *reason* for wanting a child. It is a gratuitous desire, quite
beyond reason. This is especially true if one lives the life to which
this couple has devoted itself—a life, as the girl describes it in her
moment of revulsion from it, of looking at things and trying new
drinks. In the terms that this life sets, it is entirely *un*reasonable to
want a child. But the girl has, we may say, proclaimed her emancipa-

tion from reason when she makes her remark about the hills looking like white elephants. The hills do not really look like white elephants, as the reasonable man is quick to say. They look like white elephants only if you choose to think they do, only if you think gratuitously, and with the imagination.

It is decisive in the story that the girl's simile is what it is. Some readers will have in mind the proverbial meaning of a white elephant. In certain parts of the East, this is a sacred beast; it may not be put to work but must be kept in a state at great cost. Hence we call a white elephant anything that is apparently of great value and prestige but actually a drain upon our resources of which we wish we could be rid. Quite unconsciously, the girl may be making just this judgement on the life that she and her companion have chosen. But the chief effect of the simile is to focus our attention on the landscape she observes. It has two aspects, different to the point of being contradictory. This is the first: "The girl was looking off at the line of hills. They were white in the sun and the country was brown and dry." This is the second: "The girl stood up and walked to the end of the station. Across, on the other side, were fields of grain and trees along the banks of the Ebro. Far away, beyond the river, were mountains. The shadow of a cloud moved across the field of grain and she saw the river through the trees." When she looks in one direction, she sees the landscape of sterility; when she looks in the other direction, she sees the landscape of peace and fecundity. She is aware of the symbolic meaning that the two scenes have for her, for after her second view she says, "And we could have all this . . . And we could have everything and every day we make it more impossible." It is the sudden explicitness of her desire for peace and fullness of life that makes the man's reasonable voice ring false and hollow in her ears and that leads her to her climax of desperation, her frantic request, with its seven-times repeated "please," that the man "stop talking."

It is interesting, I think, to compare the passage in the story that begins "'We want two Anis del Toro'" with the "A Game of Chess" dialogue in T.S. Eliot's "The Waste Land." Incommensurate as they are in artistic and moral intention and achievement, the story and the poem have much in common—the theme of sterility; the representation of the boredom and vacuity and desperateness of life; the sense of lost happiness not to be regained; the awareness of the failure of love; the parched, sun-dried, stony land used as a symbol of emotional desiccation, the water used as the symbol of refreshment and salvation. Like "The Waste Land," "Hills Like White Elephants" is to be read as a comment—impassioned and by no means detached—on the human condition in the modern Western world.

—Lionel Trilling, *The Experience of Literature: A Reader with Commentaries* (Garden City, NY: Doubleday and Co., 1967): 731–732

Reid Maynard on the Leitmotif of Two in "Hills Like White Elephants"

[Reid Maynard is a scholar on Henry James and Ernest Hemingway. In this excerpt he discusses the significance of scenery and the "pair" motif in "Hills Like White Elephants."]

The mountains and the river and the fields of grain are as far removed from the railway station café as the man's and girl's present strained relationship is removed from their past close relationship. When the girl wistfully views the distant scene, "the shadow of a cloud" moves "across the field of grain" and distorts the purity of her nostalgic vision, bringing her thoughts back to the sordid present. "The hills like white elephants" and other objects in the distance suggest to the girl the sensuous beauty of a love relation that is quickly deteriorating, now that she has become conscious of her lover's selfishness.

Since these images suggest the man's and the girl's past experience, they are appropriately in the background of the story's canvas. In the center of this prose painting is the railway station, where the Barcelona express stops for two minutes on its way to Madrid. The description of the station's position between the two railway lines subtly introduces the leitmotif of "two," to be reiterated in the story, but in this single instance "two" appears in an image of division or separation and suggests the actual state of the lovers; i.e., it is not an ironic "two." "Two" in "two minutes" is unobtrusively reiterated and prepares the way for the oneness, or unity, images of "two" which follow. All of these oneness or unity images operate ironically in the story, for they suggest a kind of life (symbolized by the river, mountains, and fields) which is the direct opposite of the life now being experienced by the couple. These images are of course integrated smoothly into the literal level of the story, as such symbolic images are in all of Hemingway's works. Symbols should not stand out like raisins in raisin bread, Hemingway felt.

So far, I have mentioned only two appearance of "two," both of them in the first paragraph. More such images are needed if a leitmotif strand is to be established. And they are present; "Dos cervezas," "two glasses of beer," "two felt pads," and "two anis del Toro" are images of paired objects in which the two entities of each pair are alike and, as it were, unified. These images serve as ironic contrasts to the divided couple sitting at the table, who, because of their quite different responses to life, are so unlike each other that they cannot in any sense be considered a unified pair. Not one of these "two" images would be construed as a symbol if it were seen only in terms of its literal function in an isolated context. But, collectively, the piling-up of "two" images suggest that their connotative meanings are of more significance in the story than their literal functions.

When the man callously tells the girl that her pregnancy is the only thing which has made them unhappy, the girl, deeply hurt, looks at the bead curtain and takes "hold of two of the strings of beads." Since she knows that what they once had together can never again be the same, she subconsciously reaches out to take hold of that which is lost to them. Here again their former union is suggested to the reader by the reiterated "two" motif, which at this point in the story has been established and which is now emphatically objectified, or made tangible, by the two strings of beads. And the repetition of "two" is continued in the images of "two heavy bags" and in the reappearance of "two glasses" and two "damp felt pads."

—Reid Maynard, "Leitmotif and Irony in Hemingway's 'Hills Like White Elephants'" *The University Review* 37, No. 4 (June 1971): 273–274

KENNETH G. JOHNSTON ON SETTING IN "HILLS LIKE WHITE ELEPHANTS"

[A professor of English at Kansas State University, Kenneth G. Johnston is the author of *Hemingway's 'Night Before Battle': Don Quixote, 1937*, and *The Butterfly and the Tank: Casualties of War*. In this excerpt he discusses how the setting of "Hills Like White Elephants" comments subtly on the religious tone of the story.]

Hemingway has skillfully used the setting in "Hills Like White Elephants" to help reveal and/or reinforce situation, characterization, and theme. The Spanish setting contributes to the ironic tone of the story, for the moral drama takes place in a predominantly Catholic country where the church stands in firm opposition to abortion. However, the girl does not understand Spanish, a fact which helps to reveal her essential helplessness and dependency. She is a stranger in a foreign land where her male companion is her only interpreter and guide. Their rootless existence is symbolized by the train station and by their baggage, with "labels on them from all the hotels where they spent nights." The station sits between two lines of rails, to suggest the two directions in which the couple may go—toward Madrid and the abortion, or away from Madrid toward a settled, family life. The description of the Ebro Valley, which forms the immediate background for "Hills Like White Elephants," embodies the poles of the conflict, too. It is both barren and fruitful. On the side which they sit facing, there are no trees and no shade, and in the distance the country is brown and dry; on the other side of the valley, there are "fields of grain and trees along the banks of the Ebro." Only the girl looks at the fruitful side of the valley where she glimpses the life-giving water through the trees. But as she watches the scene, "the shadow of a cloud moved across the field of grain," foreshadowing the death of the unborn child. The hills like white elephants also serve to remind us of the couple's conflicting views on abortion. A white elephant, in one meaning of the term, is anything rare, expensive, and difficult to keep; any burdensome possession; a property requiring much care and expense and yielding little profit; an object no longer esteemed by its owner though not without value to others. This is basically how the man feels about the unwanted child. On the other hand, a white elephant is also a rare pale-gray variety of Asian elephant held sacred by the Burmese and Siamese. The girl's reverence for life is captured by this meaning of the phrase. Her reluctance to have the abortion and the enormity of her sacrifice when she finally capitulates to the man's insistent demands are clearly suggested by her revealing gesture involving the beaded bamboo curtain. The beaded curtain hangs across the open door to the bar to keep out the flies, and it is repeatedly called to our attention during the story. It is the girl who first comments on the curtain, because she is curious about the Spanish words (the name of a drink) which are painted on it. A short time later, when her companion is pressuring her to submit to the operation, "the girl looked at the bead curtain, put her hand out and took hold of two of the strings of beads," as though clutching the beads of a rosary to give her the moral courage to resist. One need not argue that she is a Catholic, but this scene makes it quite clear that she is calling upon her moral and religious strength in her moment of crisis. On the other hand, the man brushes aside such considerations; at the story's end, "he went out through the bead curtain."

—Kenneth G. Johnston, *The Tip of the Iceberg: Hemingway and the Short Story* (Greenwood, FL: Penkevill Publishing Co., 1987): 127–128

DORIS LANIER ON ABSINTHE IN "HILLS LIKE WHITE ELEPHANTS"

[An assistant professor of English at Georgia Southern University, Doris Lanier is the author of *Absinthe, the Cocaine of the 19th Century*. Her articles on John Galsworthy and Mark Twain and others have appeared in *Mark Twain Journal, American Notes and Queries*, the *Markham Review,* and the *Atlanta Historical Journal.* In "The Bittersweet Taste of Absinthe in Hemingway's 'Hills Like White Elephants,'" she discusses the history and influences of absinthe in the 19th century.]

The addictive quality of the drink most certainly is meant to emphasize the addictive nature of the couple's lifestyle. Like the person addicted to absinthe, the two are addicted to a way of life that will lead to destruction—a situation that the girl is just becoming aware of. It is an empty, meaningless existence that revolves around traveling, sex, drinking, looking at things, and having pointless conversations about these things. "That's all we do, isn't it," said the girl, "look at things and try new drinks?" The lack of focus and the indirection of their lives are emphasized by the reputation of the rather indefinite "everything" and "things." When the girl says, "Everything tastes . . . like absinthe," she is making a comment about the quality of their lives and expressing her own dissatisfaction with life. When she later tells the man, "We could have everything," she is referring to those things that would bring a quality life: love, home, family. The girl is aware that "something" is missing in their lives, but she is not quite able to put that "something" into words. Neither is she able to say what "thing" will be missing if she goes through with the abortion, which is, according to the man, "the best thing to do" because the pregnancy is the "thing" that has made them unhappy. But the girl has a feeling. "I just know things," she says. Her intuitive perception of what will happen to their relationship after the abortion contrasts with his inability or unwillingness to see that their lives will be changed by the event. Though the girl would like to break the addiction and change the direction of their lives, she lacks the strength to do so without his help, and he has no desire to change.

The destructive potential of absinthe also suggests the destructive nature of the couple's relationship. Innocent-looking, seductive, and intoxicating, absinthe promises joy, excitement, heady delight, its tantalizing color and taste concealing the destructive power that is lurking in its green opulence. Subtly and slowly, however, its treacherous poison overpowers its victims, bringing with it impotence, sterility, dullness of emotions, and, finally, abject despair; likewise, the couple's illicit affair and irresponsible lifestyle, which deceptively promise joy and happiness, are fraught with concealed danger from the very beginning. It becomes a destroyer of the child, who is aborted; a destroyer of the girl, who endures the physical and emotional pain of aborting the child she wants; and a destroyer of the couple's relationship. Though the man insists that after the abortion they will be "Just like [they] were before," the girl is very aware that the abortion will probably mark the end of what had once promised to be a happy relationship. As a destroyer of life, the drink aligns itself, symbolically, with the brown, dry side of the landscape and serves to emphasize the barrenness, infertility, and unproductiveness of the couple's lives. The green color of the drink, however, reflects the greenness of the fertile landscape, a reminder that they could "have everything" instead of nothing.

Because of its reputation as an hallucinatory agent, the absinthe adds another dimension to the white elephant symbolism in the title. The hallucinatory quality of the drink relates directly to the girl's distorted view of the hills, reflecting her emotional and mental state. For the moment, at least, she is having difficulty distinguishing between illusion and reality. Her failure, or reluctance, to see the real landscape—the brown, dry hills—suggests her inability to face the reality of their deteriorating relationship. Deep down she is holding on to the belief that there is still a chance that the man will commit himself to a permanent relationship, that her pregnancy means something to him, and that she can give birth to the child that is the product of their love; in reality, however, even though he insists that he loves her and doesn't want her to do anything she doesn't want to do, he doesn't want the child and is coldly indifferent to her feelings. To him their relationship is no more than an illicit affair, a temporary arrangement; unlike the girl, he wants to avoid the possibility of a permanent relationship that would result if she had his child. By connotatively suggesting eroticism and sexual stimulation, the absinthe, like the labels on the suitcases and the girl's pregnancy, emphasizes that their relationship is mainly a sexual one.

—Doris Lanier, "The Bittersweet Taste of Absinthe in Hemingway's 'Hills Like White Elephants,'" *Studies in Short Fiction* 26, No. 3 (Summer 1989): 279–288

PAMELA SMILEY ON CONVERSATIONAL STYLES IN "HILLS LIKE WHITE ELEPHANTS"

[A professor of English at Carthage College, Pamela Smiley has written numerous articles on Mary Gordon, as well as the effects of orthodoxy on Roman Catholic women authors. In this selection she takes a linguistic approach to "Hills Like White Elephants," comparing the conversational styles of the man and the women in terms of gender.]

As the argument continues, Jig asks him whether he "wants" her to have the abortion; he translates his reply into what he "thinks," thereby denying his emotions. Directly contradicting his desire for the abortion, he twice repeats that he does not want Jig to do anything she doesn't want to do. Making several obviously impossible promises—to always be happy, to always love her, to never worry— he demonstrates flagrant bad faith. From the standard of male language these contradictions are the inevitable results of her unreasonable questions: abstract emotional responses to abstract emotional questions. From the standard of female language, they are inauthentic answers and betray trust. The differences stem from the genderlike premises that language does/does not deal with emotion and is/is not the basis of intimacy.

Jig's series of questions exposes both the American's and Jig's conversational double binds. The double bind, as described by Bateson, is a conversation with two objectives. To be true to one conversational objective a speaker must be untrue to another.

Jig's direct insistence on the American's emotional commitment forces him into a double bind. The American has two conversational objectives. The first, as Tennen phrases it, is to "Maintain camaraderie, avoid imposing and give (or at least appear to give) the other person some choice in the matter." For this reason he repeats six times within the forty-minute conversation: "I don't want you to [do anything you don't want to]." The American's other objective is the abortion. Unfortunately it is impossible to maintain easy camaraderie while insisting on the abortion. Instead of choosing one or the other, he chooses both and ignores the contradiction. While a traditional masculine standard of language might recognize the sincerity of the American's concern for Jig, the traditional feminine standard translates his contradiction as hypocrisy.

Jig is also caught in a double bind. She wants both the American and the baby. Her series of questions establishes that she can accomplish at least one of her objectives, so she releases the other with her self-sacrificing statement "I don't care about me." While Jig may be totally sincere, not caring about herself and having only the American's interests at heart, such total devotion is highly unlikely; it is more likely that she is well-taught in the skills of social deference. But in this situation, where the American's interests equal lack of growth, eternal adolescence, and sterility, her deference is self-destructive.

Of course, the unnaturalness of Jig's self-sacrifice and the artifice of her insincerity leave her vulnerable to the stereotype of "women as fickle, distrustworthy, and illogical." Judged by traditional male language patters, Jig is capricious and manipulative. Judged by traditional female language patterns, particularly within the context of the double bind, the progression of Jig's conversation is logical and inevitable.

The American's reaction to Jig's acquiescence is immediate emotional withdrawal and disavowal of responsibility for her decision or for her problem. His distance contradicts all of the protestations of love he made minutes before. It also contains a thinly veiled threat of permanent withdrawal. His knee-jerk response shows that his desire for noninvolvement and nonresponsibility is much stronger than his desire to maintain a relationship with Jig. Of course, objectively, the abortion is Jig's problem: it is her body, and the American has no right to interfere. However, the objective facts do not take into account the emotional dimension of their shared reality: the body is hers; the relationship and baby is theirs.

Even though Jig agrees to the abortion, it is obvious that she is not emotionally reconciled to it. She moves away from the table and him and, while staring at the fertile valley, continues the argument. Unwilling to give up her dream, she finds it impossible to believe he has deliberately chosen stagnation, sterility, and death. The American goes into shellshock in this segment of the conflict. While she reveals her most intimate desires, he seems to be scarcely listening.

—Pamela Smiley, "Gender-Linked Miscommunication in 'Hills Like White Elephants,'" *New Critical Approaches to the Short Stories of Ernest Hemingway,* ed. Jackson J. Benson (Durham, NC: Duke University Press, 1990): 294–296

Stanley Kozikowski on Metaphor in "Hills Like White Elephants"

[A professor of English at Bryant College, Stanley Kozikowski is a noted scholar of 19th and 20th century American literature and Tudor drama and poetry. He has published articles on Edgar Allan Poe, Henry James, and William Shakespeare in *American Transcendental Quarterly, Arizona Quarterly, Shakespeare Studies,* and elsewhere. In this excerpt he compares the importance of plot details to the man and the girl in "Hills Like White Elephants."]

To the American man, as distant from metaphor as he is from the hills, the "wind" of the hills simply defines casually and literally what an abortion is: As "the warm wind blew the bean curtain against the table," he is quick to say, "I know you wouldn't mind it, Jig. It's really not anything. It's just to let the air in ... I'll go with you ... They just let the air in and then it's perfectly natural."

Jig's reaction, delayed but deliberate, and consistent with her sense of what the hills are like, is signaled in the doorway. The wind through the bamboo curtain illustrates for her the sweet past and the bitter present. The curtain, painted with the words "Anis del Tor," signifies the sweet-now-bitter anise-seed of the bull. In the very drinks that both have, it conveys to the man, with doltish literalism, "a drink," but to Jig, a licorice taste grown as bitter as wormwood—the very taste evoking "all the things you've waited so long for, like absinthe." Jig, again figuratively, thus experiences what life—precious and unwanted—is "like." The breeze, the moving beaded curtain, and the evocative drink—like hills like white elephants—connote to Jig the sweet promise of seeding and the bitter termination of birthing. The same objects convey to the man an easy sense of exit, excision, and getting on with other things. Ever opposite, his ironic and brutal, but now figurative, words, "Oh, cut it out," are answered by Jig's sharp but now literal, "You started it"—a remarkable counterpoint of clauses, playing off his dour, unimaginative indelicacy against her superb delicacy of self-awareness.

Just as Jig holds the two strings of bamboo beads blown into her hand, she maintains full literal possession of her self and her child, as we see in the story's culminating design. But Jig nevertheless has an abortion of sorts, one precisely like hills like white elephants:

Having taken "the [not their] two bags"—"Two heavy bags" to the other side of the station, symbolically the mother and child, the man then goes into the bar from that other side, drinks "an Anis at the bar," and finally, with an astonishing irony to which he is oblivious, struts "out through the bead curtain" to the table outside, where Jig and he had sat previously, and where Jig, now smiling, remains seated. Conveyed out from the barroom, through the breezy doorway, through which the "air" gets "let in" from the other side, "the man" (appropriately nameless, mere reiterated "seed" from "bull"—Anis del toro—but now like an aerated fetus himself) is ironically terminated, expelled—in her (now triumphantly ironic figural) consciousness—from any further relationship with Jig. Clearly, Jig and her child have now come out literally "fine" after this "awfully simple operation." He, metaphorically, goes "out through the bead curtain" and out of their lives.

—Stanley Kozikowski, "Hemingway's 'Hills Like White Elephants,'" *The Explicator* 52, No. 2 (Winter 1994): 107–108

Plot Summary of
"The Short, Happy Life of Francis Macomber"

Set on an African hunting safari, "The Short, Happy Life of Francis Macomber" is similar in many respects to Hemingway's other short story of Africa, "The Snows of Kilimanjaro." Both stories are concerned with the loss and resurrection of moral manhood, with the ability of men to conquer the pressures that keep them from living free of fear and at the fullest extent of their powers. In both cases, the hero has given way to the weakening, softening influence of women and money, and in both cases the end result is death. Yet these stories are not simple tragedies. They are laced with a sense of victory, of the ability of men to triumph even over death when they have regained their manhood. "The Short, Happy Life of Francis Macomber" is also enormously ironic. Macomber dies just at the moment of his greatest triumph, and the power his wife had over him is thwarted by her own actions in attacking him.

This story is one of Hemingway's most exciting in terms of action and adventure. Based upon his own African safari in 1933 with his second wife, Pauline Pfeiffer, "The Short, Happy Life" is almost obsessively packed with figures of life and death, with the breakneck chase across the plains and deadly animals charging in surprise attacks on hunters. Yet the most important action occurs internally, within Francis Macomber's soul. Hemingway has created an emotional intensity that makes the tension of the hunt almost secondary; the contest between man and animal is merely the visible picture of the contest between Francis and his wife, Margot, as they battle for control of Macomber's life.

The action of this story takes place over a little more than 24 hours, while the "happy life" of Francis Macomber lasts rather less than 30 minutes. Francis and Margot are wealthy, young Americans who have engaged Robert Wilson as their guide on a hunting safari in Africa. The tale opens *in medias res*, on the day that Macomber and Wilson go out to shoot a lion. During the hunt, Macomber's lack of marksmanship causes him to shoot a lion in the gut, wounding but not killing it. Wilson insists that they pursue it into the brush to put it out of its misery and keep it from being a danger to people who might chance upon it. Macomber, trembling with fear, forces himself forward. There is a swishing rush through the grass, a "blood choked coughing grunt," and the lion rushes upon them. Macomber flees, "bolting like a rabbit" and leaving Wilson to shoot the lion again and again as it forces itself toward him. Hemingway has accentuated Macomber's loss of courage twice here, both in contrast to Wilson's steady shooting and against the lion's determination to attack despite its dreadful wounds. By turning tail, Francis Macomber has lost not only his manhood but his humanity.

Later in the day the Macombers and Wilson sit in camp waiting for lunch, as Margot makes scathing remarks about both her husband and the guide. She sneers at Wilson for his ugliness, both in his body and his job: "You were lovely this morning. That is if blowing things' heads off is lovely." She makes cutting remarks about Francis's inability to kill any animal that might be dangerous. Suddenly she bursts into tears and runs from the table, crying "I wish it hadn't happened. Oh, I wish it hadn't happened." When she is gone, Francis disgraces himself further by begging Wilson not to tell about the lion incident at the club frequented by game guides in Nairobi. Wilson is appalled that the man would acknowledge his cowardice so openly and resolves to have as little to do as possible with the Macombers for the rest of the trip. He will drink their whiskey but not interact socially with them.

That night Margot slips away from the tent that she shares with Francis and sleeps with Wilson, who always brings a double cot on safari in case of just such an occurrence. She has been unfaithful to her husband before but had promised to remain chaste on this trip. He lies awake in the darkness, thinking about his loss of manhood and his wife's desire to leave him. They are caught in a trap of need and weakness, she because she needs his money and her aging beauty will not allow her to find another husband if she leaves him, and he because she is still too beautiful for him to leave her.

In the morning, Francis looks at Wilson and is filled with rage, "of all the many men that he had hated, he hated Robert Wilson the most." It is here that his inner change begins. He is no longer caught in his fear and shortcomings but is able to direct his rage outward, against another man and away from the control of the woman. The three leave in the safari car to hunt buffalo, and Hemingway symbolizes the shift in their relationships by their seating in the car. During the lion hunt, Francis sat beside his wife, shrinking in embarrassment when she refused to hold his hand. Now, however, he begins to regain control and sits up front with Wilson, leaving Margot alone in the back.

They spot three bull buffalo running across the plain and give chase in the car, leaping out only at the last minute to shoot. Macomber "had no fear, only hatred of Wilson," and after shooting the first two buffalo is filled with "drunken elation." They return to the car to find Margot white and shaken, saying that she had never been more frightened in her life. Just as her husband was frightened of the charging lion, she is frightened of the terrible change in him. Many critics have seen her fear as evidence that she feels she is losing her ability to dominate him, while others have argued that she is terrified that he might be turning into the kind of thoughtless, murderous man that Wilson is. In any case, he offers her as little comfort as she did him, ignoring her terror in his desire to celebrate his newfound strength.

Margot points out that it seems unsporting to chase the buffalo from the car, and Wilson admits that it is illegal. Were she to tell the authorities in Nairobi, he would lose his license and be out of business. "Well," says Macomber, smiling at the guide's discomfiture, "Now she has something on you." As the power relations continue to shift, Margot loses her hold on Francis but manipulates Wilson under her thumb.

After killing the third buffalo, they return to where they shot the first two to find that one of the wounded bulls has run away into the brush. The situation is a perfect balance for that of the previous day: a wounded, dangerous animal lies in wait, and the two men must pursue and kill it. Yet now, instead of being the instrument of Macomber's shame, the animal is to be his yardstick of success. He feels a "wild, unreasonable happiness that he had never known before." No longer a child, he has been reborn a man. They sit in the car, with Margot hunched in the back and Francis leaning over the seat to talk excitedly to Wilson about the possibility of hunting another lion. Wilson, admiring Macomber's new demeanor, shares with him his own personal code, drawn from Shakespeare, "a man can die but once; we owe God a death and let it go which way it will, he that dies this year is quit for the next." Margot, too, recognizes the change in her husband, and sees how he has become like Wilson. "You're both talking rot. . . . Just because you've chased some helpless animals in a motor car you talk like heroes."

When they approach the undergrowth where the bull has gone, Macomber's heart is pounding again but with excitement, not fear. The bull charges, and Francis stands his ground firmly, shooting round after round into the animal's face. He sees the head lowering in surrender, and just then a white, hot light explodes in his head as a bullet from Margot's rifle tears through his brain. Hemingway is careful to point out that she "shot at the buffalo with the 6.5 Mannlicher as it seemed about to gore Macomber." It is this line that has caused the greatest controversy in the criticism of this story. Wilson assumes that she murdered her husband because she knows her dominance has been ended by his rebirth. As he says, "He *would* have left you too. . . . why didn't you poison him? That's what they do in England." Many critics have accepted Wilson's view that she was desperate to remain in control and have branded her as the ultimate in scheming, murderous women. However, Hemingway is not a writer who is careless with his words, and he states that she shot at the buffalo. If she truly wanted her husband dead, she should have let the animal gore him as it seemed about to do. By shooting him, she would lose her reputation, her freedom, and her power: everything that she needed in life. Her "victory" would be her own defeat. After her husband's death she weeps hysterically, crying out when Wilson accuses her of murder. He looks at her through his "flat blue eyes," probably remembering her comments about the illegal killing of the buffalo, and continues to torment her until she begs him to stop. In the contest for power in this story, Macomber's, though fleeting, is absolute, Wilson's is lost and regained via Margot, and she ends with only dust and ashes.

Francis Macomber's true life is exquisitely short and happy. It lasts from his transformation in the buffalo hunt until his death within the hour. Through him we see the emergence of a new level of life, a death of his fearful, animal existence as he achieves the purity of manhood and a world where the only value is courage and the only relationship worthy of interest is that between two men. The woman, who dared to trifle with men, has been punished and relegated to a subservient position, and her actions have immortalized the bravery of her husband. Although Hemingway has been criticized for his lack of character development in this tale, his ability to create emotional tension through his spare, sharp dialogue makes this one of his most successful short stories. ❁

List of Characters in
"The Short, Happy Life of Francis Macomber"

Francis Macomber is the type of the "American boy-man," the wealthy, ignorant dilettante whose name is always in the society columns. Thirty-five years old, Macomber has been married for 11 years and knows little about the "manly" rituals of the world. He knows about "duck-shooting, about fishing . . . about sex in books . . . about hanging on to his money, about most of the other things his world dealt in," yet these are not the types of knowledge Hemingway values. In many ways Francis Macomber is a parody of F. Scott Fitzgerald's glamorous Jay Gatsby, with Macomber's glamour turned to dust by his cowardice. Yet he is also a thoughtful, intelligent man who is able to face his fear and come to grips with himself in a self-searching way that accentuates his eventual bravery more than does Wilson's cheerful coldness. Throughout the story we see Macomber lose and then regain his moral manhood. Because his ceremonial triumph over fear ends so abruptly in his death, he attains a sort of glorious permanence in his pure courage.

Margot Macomber has often been seen as the typically evil, domineering woman of Hemingway's fiction. Like Brett Ashley in *The Sun Also Rises,* she is cruel and sexually promiscuous. Even her loveliness is suspect: "she had a very perfect oval face, so perfect that you expected her to be stupid." But, as Wilson suspects, she is not stupid, and her penetrating insights into those around her contrast strongly with their blindness. She sees through Wilson's pretenses and lack of morals: "you were lovely this morning. That is if blowing things' heads off is lovely," and she points out to him the immorality of chasing the buffalo from the car. Yet at the same time she is obsessed by his air of command and sleeps with him in order to punish her husband. Her marriage is a farce, she feels that she is no longer as lovely as she once was, and she is shaken by the thought that her husband's newfound courage will lead him to challenge her rule. She is cruel to both him and Wilson in the course of the story, ignoring her husband's need for support and chastising both men for their cruelty toward the animals. To characterize her as a voracious tyrant is too simplistic. Just as her husband grows in courage over the course of the story, she grows in her weakness and dependence, until in the end she is broken by her own actions and the cruel manipulation of Wilson.

The "great white hunter," *Robert Wilson* is a professional African game guide and seemingly the epitome of the Hemingwayesque hero. Free of fear and taking women only as casual sexual partners, he is the standard of masculinity and action. He brings a double cot along on his safaris so he can indulge himself with his female clients, yet he considers them a nuisance. He is possessed of a firm, simplified code of conduct: "He had his own standards about the killing and they could live up to them or get someone else to hunt for them. He knew, too, that they all respected him for this." However, Hemingway undermines this idealized portrait in several key moments. Wilson's morals do not keep him from chasing buffalo with the car and illegally threatening his employee with a lashing, nor do his skills as a hunter allow him to kill his prey cleanly or well. His lack of psychological insight leads him to misjudge both of the Macombers thoroughly, as well as bully the sobbing Margot at the end of the story.

Interestingly enough in a story about bravery, fear, and manliness, it is *the lion* that is the most obvious embodiment of courage. Shot twice in the gut, in dreadful pain and fear, the lion charges those who have caused him pain. Even when shot two more times by Wilson's enormous "cannon" of a gun, the lion crawls forward to attack. What keeps him coming is courage and desire, the two emotions that separate him from Macomber, and purity of purpose, which would be alien to Wilson's shifting, contingent moral existence. ❀

Critical Views on
"The Short, Happy Life of Francis Macomber"

WARREN BECK ON MARGOT MACOMBER

[A novelist, critic, and short story writer, Warren Beck (1896–1986) also taught English for many years at Lawrence University. His novels include *Final Score, Pause Under the Sky,* and *Into Thin Air.* He wrote critical studies of William Faulkner and James Joyce, as well as a collection of essays on Faulkner. In the essay included here, he questions the common critical opinion that Margot Macomber was a cruel, selfish murderer who killed her husband because he was in the process of shaking off her dominion.]

Presumably Wilson's stated and static idea of the predatory American female makes him suppose that what concerns Margot is the possibility of Macomber's getting out of hand, his becoming too much of a man for her to dominate. Macomber, who has not addressed his wife since he asked her if the chase wasn't marvelous and was repeatedly told she hated it, now says, "if you don't know what we're talking about why not keep out of it?" and his wife answers "contemptuously" that he'd "gotten awfully brave awfully suddenly." "But," Hemingway add pointedly, "her contempt was not secure. She was very afraid of something."

What this something may be is the crux of the matter, but there is no imperative reason for seeing it as Wilson does, especially since the story omnisciently provides other facts and suggest insights transcending Wilson's. When Macomber responds in good spirit to his wife's contemptuous remark about getting so awfully brave, and laughs, "a very natural hearty laugh," before he says, "You know I *have.* I really have," Margot "bitterly" asks, "Isn't it sort of late?" and then Hemingway opens a further perspective, far beyond Wilson's; Margot's bitterness is explained in this conspicuous interpolation: "Because she had done the best she could for many years back and the way they were together now was no one person's fault. And not when Macomber, to Margot's bitterly uttered, ironic and yet perhaps half-tentative question about its being sort of late, answers, Not for me," the woman who could be so ready when a flippant sarcasm sufficed can find nothing to say, but "sat back in the corner of the seat," in that posture not only of withdrawal but of shrinking and retreat. From something perhaps almost too big for her?

This is the last exchange between the pair. The car is driven closer to where the wounded buffalo took cover, the men get out, and Macomber, "looking back, saw his wife, with the rifle by her side, looking at him. He waved to her and she did not wave back." And then the end. And to support Wilson's suspicion that she murdered her husband there are those sharp details, the rifle handy, and she refusing to answer Macomber's confident and companionable gesture. However, Wilson has been seen plain as an uncertain spectator given to over simplification, a man of one admirable talent and only one, and beyond Wilson's cliché of Margot is much weighty evidence of a different kin—that Mrs. Macomber felt deeply her husband's failure with the lion, and passionately wishes it hadn't happened, and weeps over it, that she "had meant it to be" right on this safari, that she "had done the best she could for many years back." In this light must it not be supposed that the "something" she is "very afraid of" touches her even more closely, more personally than a danger that the maturing Macomber will leave her now?

Perhaps what Mrs. Macomber fears is a further challenge to herself as a human being and a wife, the call to try once more, to meet her husband's virtue and friendliness with a reasserted virtue and warmth of her own. Her hesitancy would then seem a quite natural reaction, compounded of an habitual negativism, the cynical pose assumed for protective coloration, plus her real disillusionment after prolonged and repeatedly defeated attempts at something better, and also perhaps a particular reluctance to confess the shabbiness of her revenge for her husband's earlier weakness. It seems conceivable, from data within the story, that Margaret Macomber is at least as good as Lady Brett Ashely, of *The Sun Also Rises*, admittedly a five-letter woman, but also on occasion one capable of deciding "not to be a bitch," being spurred to that assertion by the sight of integrity in a man. Moreover, Brett encounters another man whose standards are almost as simple as Wilson's, the hedonistic Greek count, who will drink no toasts with his wine, lest sentiment intrude upon flavor; and as Hemingway uses him to show that there is more to Brett than the count perceives, appreciative though he is, similarly the short story offers the reader more of Mrs. Macomber than is understood by Wilson, who apparently forgets or at least dismisses his momentary glimpse of what a "hell of a fine woman" she had seemed to be.

—Warren Beck, "The Shorter Happy Life of Mrs. Macomber," in *Hemingway's African Stories: The Stories, Their Sources, Their Critics*, ed. John M. Howell (New York: Charles Scribner's Sons, 1969), pp. 119–128. Originally published in *Modern Fiction Studies* 1 (November 1955): 28–37

SEAN O'FAOLAIN ON THE HEMINGWAY MYSTIQUE

[Sean O'Faolain (1900–1991) was a celebrated Irish novelist, critic, and short story writer. He was extremely active in the Irish independence movement, working as the publicity director for the Irish Republican Army, and his fictional works evoke a strong and abiding love for his country and its heritage. His works include *The Talking Tree and Other Stories, Bird Alone, The Story of Ireland, Come Back to Erin,* and an autobiography, *Vive Moi!*. In the selection below he discusses Hemingway's philosophical limitations, claiming that Hemingway should be valued more for the vigor and gallant flame of his writing.]

The Hemingway *mystique* has sometimes been called, in a superficial conversational way, a form of Stoicism. The comparison only serves to expose his shallowness. Indeed, it is to do grave injustice to Hemingway to evoke the complexity and variety of that noble philosophy, with its simultaneous belief in a wise and well-ordaining divinity and its frank acceptance of the facts of pain and practical evil; its concurrent belief in the power of the mind to control and enjoy the urges of the body, to partake in the Epicureans' "beautiful arrangement of things," and to "pass from Nature to Nature's God"; its effective blending of a life of useful activity in service to others with a quasi-Oriental love of contemplation. To invite thoughts of that full and complex *mystique* is only to be obliged to think what an unvarious wash of colour even the best of Hemingway's work has drawn across the landscape of life. We must not invite such comparisons. Hemingway is not a thoughtful man. He has no evident interest in social, moral or philosophical ideas at all. He is not and never pretended to be an intellectual. He is a man who loves gallant men and gallant animals. He is also a man, and it is this which gives him his real stature also as an artist, who loves the gallant spirit, and he has roved the world in search of that flame of the spirit in men and beasts. To capture that flame, to record the moments in which it burns most brightly, has been his life's design. But to explain to us the origins of such moments, to give us their pedigree, is beyond his power. So, as to the psychological reasons why Francis Macomber did not grow up to be a Jordan, or why Jordan did not grow up to be a Francis Macomber, he has not even the inkling of an idea. How could he, having so early decided to confiscate that element of past Time during which men are made whatever they finally are at the testing-hour.

—Sean O'Faolain, "Ernest Hemingway, or Men Without Memories," *The Vanishing Hero, Studies in Novelists of the Twenties* (London: Eyre and Spottiswoode, 1956), pp. 135–166

℘

JOSEPH DEFALCO ON COLOR IN "THE SHORT, HAPPY LIFE OF FRANCIS MACOMBER"

[Joseph DeFalco is an important critic of Edgar Allan Poe and Ernest Hemingway, as well as other American writers. His has contributed to *Literature and Psychology, Walt Whitman Review,* and other journals, and edited the collected poems of Christopher Pearse Cranch. In this selection, taken from his book *The Hero in Hemingway's Short Stories,* DeFalco provides a Freudian reading of color symbolism in "The Short, Happy Life of Francis Macomber."]

When Macomber can express moral outrage, he has taken a first step toward manhood. Hemingway has already interjected a detail which foreshadows such a step, and, in fact, it is part of the controlling symbol of the story. While Macomber's wife has been with Wilson, Macomber has been reliving the whole experience of his flight of cowardice from the lion. And, too, just before the wife returns to the tent, Macomber has a dream which signals his coming change of character: "It was now about three o'clock in the morning and Francis Macomber, who had been asleep a little while after he had stopped thinking about the lion, wakened and then slept again, woke suddenly, frightened in a dream of the bloody-headed lion standing over him." The lion becomes in this sequence the manifestation of Macomber's cowardice, and its appearance in the dream represents the force which must be overcome.

The lion becomes the totemistic symbol of both the father-authority, the lover of the mother-wife, and the symbol of the new self which Macomber must become in order to usurp the father's couch. The appearance of the bloody head further suggests the guilt feelings such an ordeal necessarily arouses. Wilson is the human personification of the traits which the lion incorporates, and always he is described with reference to the color red—a symbol of passion and vitality. For example, Mrs. Macomber refers to him as "the beautiful red-faced Mr. Robert Wilson;" and Macomber says to his wife at one point: "'I hate that red-faced swine.'" The narrative description also refers to Wilson many times by use of the color: "He was about middle height with sandy hair, a stubby mustache, a very red face and extremely cold blue eyes." When Mrs. Macomber holds her husband in contempt and looks to Wilson as the husband-surrogate, Hemingway marks the attachment with further color symbolism by associating Mrs. Macomber with a near-color of red: "The rose-colored, sun-proofed shirt she wore," or "looking pretty rather than beautiful in her faintly rosy khaki." When Macomber later gains his courage, a fact which his wife cannot reconcile, she is described several times over as "white-faced." By use of the color device, Hemingway thus paints in thin outline the passing of courage and vitality—the blood of the lion—from Wilson and Mrs. Macomber to Macomber.

—Joseph DeFalco, *The Hero in Hemingway's Short Stories* (Pittsburgh: University of Pittsburgh Press, 1963): 204–205

PHILIP YOUNG ON MANLINESS IN "THE SHORT, HAPPY LIFE OF FRANCIS MACOMBER"

[A professor of American literature at Pennsylvania State University, Philip Young (1918–1991) wrote several books and articles on modern American authors, including *Hawthorne's Secret: An Untold Tale* and *The Private Melville*. He also edited *The Hemingway Manuscripts: An Inventory*, and wrote a psychobiographical study of the author entitled *Ernest Hemingway*. In this excerpt he interprets "The Short, Happy Life of Francis Macomber" as a description of how men learn the code of honor, or manliness, from each other.]

These distinctions between the hero and his tutor—the man whom the hero emulates, who has the code he would like to operate by, too—clarify and enrich a couple of Hemingway's later, best, and best-known stories, "The Short, Happy Life of Francis Macomber," and "The Snows of Kilimanjaro." These long pieces are both clearly ritualistic—one a ceremonial triumph over fear, the other a rite in which a part of the self is destroyed. They present certain difficulties, however, because of new approaches the author took to his material and his protagonists.

Hemingway distinguished between "true" and "made up" stories. Both of these, though they use a great deal of autobiography, are of the latter type. These are personal stories, but they are not literal once: in Africa in the thirties Hemingway did not die of an infection, nor was he chased by a lion and murdered by his wife. The protagonists are also "made up" in that in each of the stories the writer adopted a mask that is for once grotesque, incongruous and truly a distortion. Both Macomber and Harry (in "Kilimanjaro") exaggerate some of the hero's weaknesses, failing, shortcomings. Harry is a failure as a man and as a writer; Macomber is a coward. It is very much as if Hemingway was getting rid of things again, but here he took a new and hypercritical attitude toward his protagonists. These men are not wholly unfamiliar as leading players in Hemingway, but they are outside the pattern he built in that they are seen through a glass very darkly or, to put it more cogently, they are seen in a glass—as in a Coney Island funhouse—which mirror into magnified prominence the growing paunch, the receding hairline, the sagging muscles.

"The Short, Happy Life" is, among other things, a detailed description of the process of learning the code and its value. Macomber, a frightened man, is seen in the story learning the code from Wilson, his professional hunting guide. He is presented as being very ignorant at first, but he painfully learns and he becomes a man in the process. Before that happens, however, it is apparent that Hemingway was using this plot of instruction in courage and honor to comment, as he had not done to this extent before, on many other things. The story is, for example, an analysis of the relationship between the sexes in America, and the relationship is in the nature of declared warfare.

—Philip Young, *Ernest Hemingway: A Reconsideration* (University Park, PA: The Pennsylvania State University Press, 1966): 69–70

⊛

SHERIDAN BAKER ON HEMINGWAY'S AUTOBIOGRAPHICAL ELEMENTS IN "THE SHORT, HAPPY LIFE OF FRANCIS MACOMBER"

[Sheridan Baker's teaching career included positions at the University of Michigan and the University of Nagoya, Japan. He was awarded the Explicator Prize and is a past president of the Michigan Academy of Science, Arts and Letters. Professor Baker is the author of *The Practical Stylist, The Essayist,* and *The Complete Stylist.* Together with Northrup Frye and George Perkins, he edited *The Practical Imagination* and the *Harper Handbook to Literature.* He has published poetry in *The New Yorker, Epoch,* and other magazines. In this selection, taken from his book *Ernest Hemingway: An Introduction and Interpretation,* Baker explores the autobiographical elements of "The Short, Happy Life of Francis Macomber."]

As in *Green Hills* and "The Snows," Africa and its British stand as indictments of American society. Wilson lives by "good form." Bravery is no problem: one simply does what a man ought. Wilson is the prime exhibit of Hemingway's "Code Hero," a man less frequent and complete in Hemingway than the label suggests—a label that has nicely confused the issue as to who is here and what is code. America has lost the bravery Wilson personifies. The glittering American female has softened the men into boys, or picked them soft. But it does not matter when you die but how well, like the dying lion, recast from Hemingway's thoughts in *Green Hills,* digging his claws in.

The story reaches visibly back through *Green Hills.* Wilson is a shorter, younger, redder Pop, with the same phrases, the same husky voice; and with Pop's fatherly affection turned to an admiring and hostile adultery. Margot Macomber has Mrs. Hemingway's wit, brightness, and dark hair. But she is enameled with malice, and takes her name from some beautiful Margot of the Hemingways' acquaintance, mentioned as they discuss Pop's pulchritude. And the very tall, crew-cut Macomber, athlete and sportsman, the all-American boy of thirty-five, has a great deal of Hemingway in him in spite of the Princeton physique. Their ages are almost identical: during his African trip Hemingway was six months short of his thirty-fifth birthday, and he wrote the story when he was thirty-six. Like Hemingway, Macomber is good with a Springfield. From British Wilson, Macomber hears the lines from *Henry IV* that Hemingway's admired British friend, Captain Eric Edward Dorman-Smith, of His Majesty's Fifth Fusiliers, had written out for him in Milan—lines that Hemingway took as "a permanent protecting talisman," as he says in his "Introduction" to *Men at War:* "A man can die but once; we owe God a death . . . he that dies this year is quit for the next." Hemingway has thought affectionately of Dorman-Smith, "old chink," toward the end of *Green Hills:* "Pop and chink were much alike."

—Sheridan Baker, *Ernest Hemingway: An Introduction and Interpretation* (New York: Holt, Rinehart and Winston, 1967): 99–100

⊛

JOHN S. HILL ON WILSON AND IRONY IN "THE SHORT, HAPPY LIFE OF FRANCIS MACOMBER"

[Chairman of the English honors program at Illinois State University, John S. Hill has contributed articles to *The Southern Humanities Review, American Notes and Queries,*

The Huntington Library Quarterly, and other journals. In this excerpt he contrasts the characterization of Robert Wilson to that of Margot Macomber in "The Short, Happy Life of Francis Macomber," explaining Hemingway's use of understatement and irony.]

Robert Wilson is very much the Hemingway hero. His independence, his reliance on his own powers resemble those of Hemingway himself in *Green Hills of Africa* (1934) and those of Harry Morgan in *To Have and Have Not* (1937, a year after "Macomber" was published). Thus Wilson is fit to be the spokesman at the end of the story. He explains the shooting through the use of irony and understatement. If the reader misses this point, he will not understand the ending.

The title itself supports this fact. Francis Macomber's "short happy life" begins when he finds he has conquered fear and ends when his wife accidentally kills him. This final interval in his life, although factually "happy," is very ironically "short" in view of what Francis's life would have been had he lived. The irony is much like "the irony of fate," for at the moment Macomber realizes happiness he is destroyed. Again, in view of what Macomber's life would have been, the title is rich in understatement.

Wilson uses understatement earlier in the story. When Margaret runs off crying, he murmurs, "Women upset." When Francis discovers courage, that "wild unreasonable happiness that he had never known before," Wilson says merely, "Cleans out your liver." The use of irony is strongest when Wilson says, attempting to cover Macomber's cowardice with a laugh, "You know in Africa no woman ever misses her lion and no white man ever bolts." The irony is evident: Francis did bolt; Margaret will indeed miss her target.

Wilson's use of irony must be considered at the climax if we are to understand the story's ending. Now, the climax involves Margaret's act of shooting, which is important in two respects: one, she kills Francis just as he is about to triumph; this is one more instance of her keeping him from being triumphant at any time. Second, it stresses her irresponsibility. She shoots from the car, although she knows this is illegal. She shoots although she knows little about guns—she uses a 6.5 mm. rifle to shoot at a buffalo, which is like trying to kill a moose with a .22. In short, her act of shooting emphasizes her utter irresponsibility about anything important.

—John S. Hill, "Robert Wilson: Hemingway's Judge in 'Macomber,'"
The University Review 35, No. 2 (Winter 1968): 129–132

☙

NINA BAYM ON MARGOT MACOMBER AND THE LION IN "THE SHORT, HAPPY LIFE OF FRANCIS MACOMBER"

[Nina Baym is one of the best-known feminist scholars in America, as well as a noted scholar of American literature. She has received fellowships from the Guggenheim Foundation and the National Endowment for the Humanities, and has been an associate of the Center for Advanced Studies at Princeton University. Since 1963 she has been a Liberal Arts and Sciences Jubilee Professor of English at the University of Illinois at Urbana-Champaign. She is the author of *The Shape of Hawthorne's Career, Women's Fiction: A Guide to Novels By and About Women, 1820-1870,* and *Feminism and American Literary History: Essays.* She is the co-editor of the *Norton Anthology of American Literature* and the *Columbia History of the United States.* In this essay she discusses the relationship between Margot Macomber and the lion in "The Short, Happy Life of Francis Macomber."]

Now, if we move forward again to Margot Macomber who is sitting in the car during the buffalo chase, we see her in process of seeing that "there was no change in Wilson. She saw Wilson as she had seen him the day before when she had first realized what his great talent was. But she saw the change in Francis Macomber now." What was it that Margot, the day before, had realized Wilson's "great talent" to be? It was his talent for "blowing things' heads off." We might surmise that Margot sees in her husband the process of transformation into a man like Wilson. "You're both talking rot," said Margot. "Just because you've chased some helpless animals in a motor car you talk like heroes," she says, including both of them in her assessment.

If it is true that Macomber is becoming another Wilson, and that Margot is aware of it, then her attempt to save her husband from the buffalo at just that moment becomes a quixotic act that may even be called heroic. Certainly her interests coincide with those of the animals, not with men of Wilson's sort. That in shooting to save her husband from the buffalo she has acted against her own interests is made clear by the story's trick ending, and of course it is a trick, in the tradition of Guy de Maupassant, when the intended act backfires—one might say literally backfires—in every respect.

Before the incident with the lion, Margot Macomber has not been hostile to hunting: "'You'll kill him marvelously,' she said, 'I know you will. I'm awfully anxious to see it.'" She comes to hate hunting when she sees what it consists of. She sees that Macomber, with Wilson and his gun behind him, is never in any real danger. And she sees that what is a matter of life and death for the animal becomes a wasteful war game for men. The story quietly endorses her judgment by giving the lion himself the last word on his wounding and death:

> That was the story of the lion. Macomber did not know how the lion had felt before he started his rush, nor during it when the unbelievable smash of the .505 with a muzzle velocity of two tons had hit him in the mouth, nor what kept him coming after that, when the second ripping crash had smashed his hind quarters and he had come crawling on toward the crashing, blasting thing that had destroyed him. Wilson knew something about it and only expressed it by saying "damned fine lion."

Macomber knew nothing about the lion; Wilson knew something, but a good deal less than he thought; Margot knows almost everything. But Margot does not recognize, it seems safe to say, that she too, in relation to these men, is in the situation of the lion—imaged as dangerous, but in fact helpless. I am not saying that Margot "should" have let the buffalo kill her husband, nor do we know what would have happened if she had held her fire. Strictly speaking, we cannot even speculate on this matter since these are not real events and since they are narrated to the end of this conclusion and no other. The point is that whatever she does, Margot is as "buffaloed" as the buffalo. She has an illusion of power which she exercises in occasional infidelities to her husband, but such exercises rather than freeing her deliver her from the power of one man to the power of another. Yet when she acts for her husband instead of against him, she is no better off.

—Nina Baym, "'Actually, I Felt Sorry for the Lion.'" *New Critical Approaches to the Short Stories of Ernest Hemingway*, ed. Jackson J. Benson (Durham, NC: Duke University Press, 1990): 118–119

Blythe and Sweet on Robert Wilson in "The Short, Happy Life of Francis Macomber"

[Hal Blythe and Charlie Sweet are professors of English at Eastern Kentucky University. They have collaborated on articles on John Cheever, Bobbie Ann Mason, James Joyce, T. S. Eliot, and others. In this article they investigate Robert Wilson's motivation in "The Short, Happy Life of Francis Macomber" and paint a picture of him as a deliberately Machiavellian conspirator.]

Wilson indeed lures Macomber to his death, and the act is calculated. Wilson deliberately exposes Macomber to the greatest possible danger. Wilson figures that at the very least while Macomber is trying for the most difficult shot, the buff may gore him to death, leaving one less witness to the motor car indiscretion. Compare this advice to Wilson's directions to Macomber before the lion hunt wherein the guide tells him to shoot at one hundred yards or less for then "You can hit him wherever you want at that." Clearly with the lion there is no implied challenge or degree of difficulty. In short, Wilson knows Macomber's preoccupation with shooting the buffalo with the tricky nose shot could result in Macomber's immediate death by goring or something even more advantageous to the guide.

Next, Wilson, who has previously taken most of his bearers on the hunt, chooses only one boy, using the weak excuse, "The other can watch to keep the birds away." The guide is aware that one bearer, providing less distraction, affords a clearer shot from the car.

Other details suggest the intricacy of Wilson's plan. The two hunters dismount from the car. Hemingway notes that Macomber "saw his wife, with the rifle by her side, looking at him." Pro that he is, Wilson knows the wounded buff will charge, and when it does, he kneels, making himself a very small target from the car; even Macomber at this point is unable to see his guide. Wilson shoots at the buffalo, more than once, but doesn't drop it; for a professional hunter, this poor aim must be deliberate (he stopped the lion immediately). Finally, right before the fatal shot, Wilson not coincidentally ducks to one side; why, if not getting himself out of the way while simultaneously offering Margot a clearer line of fire from the car?

It is also important to note here that Wilson knows Margot will shoot in these circumstances. He has seen the rift develop between husband and wife, he understands what has kept them together, he has seen Margot's control over her husband diminish with Macomber's sudden maturation, and he has verbally widened the gap between them. Knowing Margot has a motive, Wilson, then, has simply provided her with the means (the light Mannlicher) and the opportunity (he even has the car parked near the brush to provide a close shot).

The aftermath of the shooting further emphasizes a deliberate plan on Wilson's part. Margot is crying hysterically, Macomber is dead, and Wilson, showing no sign of remorse, calmly gives orders. In rapid succession he tells Margot not to touch the body and to get in the car; he instructs the gunbearer to leave the death weapon alone and fetch a witness. Immediately, Wilson begins to seize control back from Margot. He sarcastically pronounces the fatal shooting an "accident." But instead of comforting her, the normal human reaction in such a situation, he explains the upcoming inquest and suggests the motive the authorities might find ("He *would* have left you") Wilson reiterates the word "accident," employing the trigger word "Nairobi." His subtext is subtle, but clear; now she will be on trial for misconduct there, not he.

The cleverness and thoroughness of Wilson's plan are unmistakable. In a very short time he has turned the tables on his would-be controller. He has changed the very instrument of his disadvantage—a motor car wrongfully used for shooting—into the instrument of his advantage: in a total role reversal, the very thing that Margot would have held over his head to the authorities he now holds over her—she has shot wrongfully from a car. To emphasize this mastery he forces her at the end to beg. "Please, please stop it," she implores. Illustrating the power he now holds, he underscores her capitulation with "Please is much better." The consummate hunter has bagged his game.

—Hal Blythe and Charlie Sweet, "Wilson: Architect of the Macomber Conspiracy," *Studies in Short Fiction* 28, No. 3 (Summer 1991): 305–310

Plot Summary of
"The Snows of Kilimanjaro"

Hemingway often referred to "The Snows of Kilimanjaro" as his favorite short story and once admitted that he "never wrote so directly about (himself) as in that story." At the time Hemingway wrote "Snows," he had not written seriously in over three years and had become fearful that he would die before accomplishing his literary aspirations. To some extent even the plot of the story echoes Hemingway's life. During a safari to Africa in 1934, he became gravely ill with amoebic dysentery, and his rescue plane flew out past the majestic bulk of Mt. Kilimanjaro. This story is the tale of Hemingway as he might have been had he given in to sloth, to riches, to the barrenness of mind that can accompany much luxury. It is the story of the conflict every artist faces between idealism and the seductions of the world, between the lonely work to create worlds in words, and the lazy pleasures of the flesh.

The action of this story, unlike "The Short, Happy Life of Francis Macomber," Hemingway's other African story, is entirely internal. Perhaps in a reaction to his own increasing fame as a "man of action," Hemingway emphasizes the role of memory and analysis, the essential tools of a writer. As an experiment in psychological motivation and inner conflict, "Snows" is one of Hemingway's greatest triumphs.

The protagonist of "Snows" is Harry, a writer who has abandoned his craft to live a life of aimless pleasure, marrying ever richer women as his drive to write fades away. This theme, of the woman who destroys man's virility through the smothering pressure of home comfort, is a common one in Western literature. Hemingway later acknowledges, through Harry, that such an attitude is merely a ploy on the part of the man to escape responsibility for his actions. Harry has come to Africa to "work the fat off his soul" by living in Spartan hunting camps. Two weeks prior to the story he scratched his leg on a thorn, and his neglect of the problem led to an infection. The story opens as he lies on a cot, dying of gangrene in his right leg. "The marvelous thing is that it's painless," he says, "That's how you know when it starts." He is referring to the deadly infection but also to the rot in his soul. When he chose to let life become painless, when he neglected his talent, his literary self began to die.

Harry stares out at the vultures gathered around the camp as he quarrels with his wife, Helen. These vultures, like the hyena later in the story, are symbols of death, of the impossibility of Harry's recovery. He looks at them and realizes that "he would never write the things that he had saved to write. . . . Well, he would not have to fail at trying to write them either." Part of his remorse springs from his acknowledgment that it was fear that held him back as well as laziness. He was afraid that he did not have the talent and thus was unable to create the talent within himself. At this point Hemingway switches to italics, as Harry reminisces about his skiing vacations and war experiences in the Austrian Alps. It is in these italicized interior monologues that Hemingway shows what Harry should have written about, the beauty, vigor, and heroism of his life that is in violent contrast to his present immobility and corruption.

When Harry awakens he attacks his wife again, telling her that he never loved her. She cries, and he relents, telling her "You know I love you." But this is only the "familiar lie he made his bread and butter by." Even love, the driving force in so many of Hemingway's works, is deadened and lost. He thinks back to the way he lived his life, how the comfort dulled his ability and will to work. In his mind, he calls his wife "this rich bitch, this kindly caretaker and destroyer of his talent." But in a moment of candor he recognizes that he had destroyed his talent himself, that there is no one to blame for his decay but his own neglect.

As he lies on his cot, drinking whiskey and soda with Helen, Harry feels his anger at himself fading away. He no longer sees Helen as a destroyer but as a good woman. Just then, as he has begun to slip into his old habits of mind, he feels death approaching in a rush. It is like the hyena he had just seen slipping by the tent, a "sudden evil-smelling emptiness" that floods upon him. He flinches and retreats again into his memories of youth. In his dreams he brawls in the street over a woman, makes love in the cool of night, and strolls by the cafés of Paris. "He had been in it and he had watched it and it was his duty to write of it; but now he never would." In a last effort to be true to his art, to pour our his memories into writing, he asks Helen if she could take dictation. But she never learned, and he is left to his memories.

He thinks of his youth in the mountains, picking blackberries and playing in the woods. Like Harry's other flashbacks, this is a reference to Hemingway's own childhood, to stories Hemingway himself had not told. Just as the skiing trip is the story of Hemingway's visit to Austria with his wife, the cabin in the wood is that of his grandfather in Petoskey, Michigan. The contrast is clear; whereas Harry's memories are caught silently in his mind, Hemingway has transformed them into fiction into the beauty of the written text.

Harry looks at Helen's face in the firelight, hearing the hyena scuffling behind her in the darkness. To him she is the symbol of luxury and the loss of his soul. He looks at her and hears the hyena, the natural emblem of death. He feels death approaching, closer and closer until he feels its weight pressing upon his chest. He cannot move or speak, and as it crouches upon him the camp workers lift his cot, and he feels the weight leaving him. In truth it is not the weight of death leaving him but the last of his life flickering away. As he dies, he becomes lost in a vision. Unlike his previous imaginings, this one is not set off in italics, it is a part of his present life. He imagines that morning has come and with it a rescue plane to fly him to the hospital in Nairobi. Death arrives in the form of the pilot, Compton. He smiles, always a gentleman, and tells Harry that there is room only for one in the plane. He will come back for Helen, obviously when it is her time to die. As they fly through the air, Harry looks down on the fields and grazing herds of Africa, the light and sparkling life of the plains. The sky darkens as if with storm clouds, until they climb to the east, the direction from which light comes, and break free into view of the flashing white top of Kilimanjaro.

Just then, back at the camp the hyena breaks forth in a "strange, human, almost crying sound." Helen awakens and cries out as she sees Harry's motionless form, his leg hanging grotesquely free of its wrappings.

Harry's final vision of Kilimanjaro is troubling for many critics. It refers back to the epigraph at the beginning of the story, in which Hemingway mentions the carcass of a leopard that was found frozen and dried at the mountain's peak. The cold, pure heights of the mountain, in which the leopard achieves a type of immortality due to its inconceivable persistence, contrast sharply with the heat and stench of the plain where Harry lies dying, haunted by the skulking hyena. Yet Harry has not earned his vision. He did not have the courage to venture into the heights of his profession to seek immortality as did the leopard. Instead, he fed off the wealth of his wives, preying on them like a jackal or a hyena. His redemption seems false, as though Hemingway could not bear to condemn his own alter ego to failure. Yet by putting the final vision in roman type rather than italics, Hemingway may be indicating that Harry has finally created something, he has forsworn his prior life in the moment of death. The flight of his soul brings him to a visionary epiphany, yet this bittersweet ending refuses to accord Harry the permanence of the leopard's triumph. ❀

List of Characters in
"The Snows of Kilimanjaro"

In many ways *Harry* is a terrible vision of Hemingway as he might have been, the failed writer living a life of purposeless sensuality in the cradle of wealth. As was Hemingway, he is wounded in the knee, and he must be flown out of the plains past Mt. Kilimanjaro, just as Hemingway was in 1934 when he was deathly ill with amoebic dysentery. Yet Harry is what Hemingway was emphatically not: a failed writer. In his youth Harry traveled around Europe and lived his life with vigor and daring, but since then he has become slothful and has destroyed his talent with drink, laziness, and betrayal. Two weeks ago he scratched his knee on a thorn bush, and the cut developed into the gangrene that is eating away his leg. Harry is the perfect image of the artist ruined by indulgence in the world, the living man who is as dead spiritually as his rotten leg is dead physically.

Harry's wife, *Helen*, is a figure of pathos. Rich and good in bed, yet at the same time intellectually boring and overbearingly maternal, she is everything Hemingway most feared in a woman. She is unfailingly kind to her husband despite his verbal cruelty and petulance. Her first husband died when she was young, leaving her with two grown children who were embarrassed by her attention. She consoled herself with drink and lovers until one of her children was killed in a plane crash, at which point she became terribly afraid of being alone. Hemingway stresses her wealth and leisurely lifestyle, her traveling from one resort town to the next. To him she is as much a symbol of death as the hyena because it is her type of wealth and luxury that kills talent. When Harry looks at her "well-known, pleasant smile, he felt death come again."

The *leopard*, whose frozen carcass is found dried in the perennial snows of Mt. Kilmanjaro's summit, is everything that Harry could have been but was not. Its heroic, single-minded perseverance led it to the mountaintop, just as Harry's talent could have led him to the achievement of his literary dreams. Yet while Harry's slothfulness condemns him to the hot stench of the plains and the realm of the skulking hyena, the leopard achieves immortality in the cold, pure snows. If Harry is the death in life of gangrene and wasted talent, and Helen is the death in life of suffocating materialism, the leopard is the life in death of one whose accomplishments gain perpetual fame. ❀

Critical Views on
"The Snows of Kilimanjaro"

CHARLES CHILD WALCUTT ON HARRY AND THE
LEOPARD IN "THE SNOWS OF KILIMANJARO"

[A professor of English for many years at Queens College
and the Graduate School and University Center of the City
University of New York, Charles Child Walcutt (1908–1989)
was the author of *Man's Changing Mask: Modes and
Methods of Characterization in Fiction* and other works on
modern and American literature, as well as the editor of
Anatomy of Prose. He is also well-known as a pioneer in new
methods of teaching basic reading, such as the phonics
system. The selection below, in which Walcutt compares
Harry to the leopard, has been enormously influential in all
subsequent readings of this short story.]

I believe the leopard in "The Snows of Kilimanjaro" is a symbol of
Harry's moral nature.

The conflict upon which the story turns is the conflict in Harry's
life between a fundamental moral idealism (Hemingway would not
call it that, of course; he might call it an impulse toward Truth, or
perhaps merely a basic integrity) and the corrupting influence of
aimless materialism. By aimless materialism I mean, first, that to
people of the 20's like Harry, the language and concepts of conven-
tional morality had been exposed as pious fraud. They had taken us
into a war and had brought us out of it without ever coming to grips
with "reality." The disillusion of Harry's generation led to cynicism
and self-indulgence. Morally defrauded, they attempted to escape all
values by plunging into sensation, drink, violence. The plunge was
never complete and never satisfying, for it was essentially *desperate.*

This desperation, with Harry, is revealed by the dying reveries in
which he shows how he has, again and again, searched human
nature, respected human integrity, pitied human suffering. He has,
in short, lived with an impulse toward truth, an obscure respect for
man, and a sense of human dignity and integrity that constitute a set
of values. And the substance of his reveries as he lies dying, shows
that what he regrets most is his failure to record his perceptions of

human dignity and integrity. If he could have done so he might have contributed some slight bit to the improvement of man's lot.

On the surface, however, Harry has trifled cynically with his life; he has wasted his vitality. Gazing on the white peak of Kilimanjaro, he sees a symbol there of Truth, meaning,—or an incarnation of the ideal. The mountain represents the undefined ideal for which he has struggled. From a purely naturalistic point of view, it is illogical that Harry should have such ideals, for they are not fond in or justified by the environment in which he has lived. It is just as naturalistically illogical that Harry should continue to believe in man and search for meanings and values as that a purely predatory leopard should climb up into the frozen desert toward the top of the mountain. What drove the leopard up there is a mystery. It is the same sort of mystery as the force that keeps idealism alive in Harry. All reason, in a predatory world, is against it, but there it is.

—Charles Child Walcutt, "Hemingway's 'The Snows of Kilimanjaro,'"
The Explicator 7, No. 6 (April 1949): item 43

(%)

CARLOS BAKER ON SYMBOLS IN "THE SNOWS OF KILIMANJARO"

> [A Woodrow Wilson Professor of English at Princeton University, Carlos Baker (1909–1987) is the author of several works on Ernest Hemingway, including *Hemingway, the Writer as Artist, Ernest Hemingway: A Life Story,* and a collection of Hemingway's correspondence. He has also published two novels, a collection of poetry, and a critical study of Emerson. In this selection he discusses why Hemingway uses the symbols he does in "The Snows of Kilimanjaro."]

The story is technically distinguished by the operation of several natural symbols. These are non-literary images, as always in Hemingway, and they have been very carefully selected so as to be in complete psychological conformity with the locale and the dramatic situation. How would the ideas of death and of immortality present themselves in the disordered imagination of a writer dying of gangrene as he waits for the plane which is supposed to carry him out of the wilderness to the Nairobi hospital? The death-symbols were relatively easy. Every night beasts of prey killed grazing animals and left the pickings to those scavengers of carrion, the vultures and the hyenas.

It is entirely natural that Harry, whose flesh is rotting and noisome—is, in fact, carrion already—should associate these creatures with the idea of dying. As he lies near death in the mimosa shade at the opening of the story, he watches the birds obscenely squatting in the glare of the plain. As night falls and the voice of the hyena is heard in the land, the death-image transfers itself from the vultures to this other foul devourer of the dead. With the arrival of his first strong premonition of death, which has no other form than "a sudden, evil-smelling emptiness," Harry finds without astonishment that the image of the hyena is slipping lightly along the edge of the emptiness. "Never believe any of that," he tells his wife, "about a scythe and a skull." His mind has been far away in the days of his former life in Paris, and now it has come back to Africa. "It can be two bicycle policemen as easily, or be a bird. Or it can have a wide snout like a hyena." Death has just come as if to rest its head on the foot of the cot, the direction from which the infection will rise up towards the vital center. Presently it moves in on him, crouching on his chest so that he cannot breathe.

Harry's dying directive, "Never believe any of that about a scythe and a skull," is an important commentary on Hemingway's own habitual approach to the development of natural symbols. He is prepared to use, where they conform to the requirements of an imaginary situation, any of the more ancient symbols—whether the threes and nines of numerology, or the weight of the Cross in Christian legend. But the scythe and the skull, though ancient enough, simply do not fit the pattern of Harry's death and are therefore rejected in favor of the foul and obscene creatures which have now come to dominate Harry's imagination.

—Carlos Baker, *Hemingway, the Writer as Artist* (Princeton: Princeton University Press, 1956): 193–194

MARION MONTGOMERY ON THE LEOPARD AND THE HYENA IN "THE SNOWS OF KILIMANJARO"

[A professor of English at the University of Georgia, Marion Montgomery is the recipient of an Earhart Foundation grant for his critical works, as well as the Georgia Writer's Association Award for his 1964 novel *Darrell*. He has published several novels and volumes of poetry, as well as critical studies of Ezra Pound, Dante, and Wordsworth. In this selection he compares Harry to the leopard and the hyena, finding that Harry's final moments allow him to escape the psychological death and rot that the hyena represents.]

Harry is, by this time, approaching a moral rejuvenation through self-condemnation. He has come to Africa in the first place to work the fat off body and soul, to give up the easy comforts in an attempt to regain the old hunting form, and it is a wry irony of fate that threatens to destroy him before he can reclaim himself. But in spite of fate, he begins an affirmation. Now rejecting the code of life corresponding to the hyena's in the animal world, he reaffirms that corresponding to the leopard's. He summons memories to strengthen him. There are his grandfather's guns, burned when the family cabin burned. His grandfather, he recalls, refused to let the boy disturb them in their ashes. The image of the burned guns in ashes suggests the leopard of the headnote: there is an unexplained steadiness of devotion in the old man's attitude that is of the same order as that which led the leopard beyond its element. Harry remembers, too, his destitute neighbors in the Place Contrescarpe where he lived before he began living the lie. He recalls those drunkards who killed their poverty with drink and the "sportifs" who "took it out in exercising" by bicycle racing. Here are the hyenas and leopards of the Paris slum, and Harry, in his reflections, judges the drunkards much as he judges Barker and himself and the hyena. He remembers the half-wit chore boy in Wyoming who remained constant to duty to the point of foolishly shooting a man to protect some hay, and there is in Harry's remembering a note of approval of the boy's action. The full-hearted deed is important to him, not the consequences of appearing ridiculous by defending burnt guns or winning third prize in a bicycle race, or being jailed, perhaps hanged, for shooting a man, or ending up with an Armenian whore instead of a respectable wife.

When his present wife interrupts these reflections of past events to bring Harry more broth, to insist that he do what is good for him, he resists her, more determined than ever, because what she means by *good* is, to Harry, *easy*. Death is Harry's chance of self-recovery. He will not care for death, he reflects, and thus he will overcome it. He is determined he won't spoil this experience as he has so many others. He fears only pain, not the idea, and the pain itself does not bother him now. He drifts into death thinking that he has waited too long and too late, and that his life is therefore wasted. "The party's over and you are with your hostess now." But he is bored with his hostess death. "He looked at her [wife's-death's] face between him and the fire . . . He heard the hyena make a noise." He feels death creep up his leg again and "he could smell its breath." It had no shape. "It simply occupied space," negative being. "You've got a hell of a breath," says Harry, his last words as he feels death crouching on his chest. Then he has the sensation of the cot's being lifted as he is carried into the tent, after which everything becomes "all right." His last thoughts show no fear.

—Marion Montgomery, "The Leopard and the Hyena: Symbol and Meaning in 'The Snows of Kilimanjaro,'" *University of Kansas City Review* 27, No. 4 (June 1961): 277–282

☙

ROBERT WOOSTER STALLMAN ON HARRY'S INTERIOR MONOLOGUES IN "THE SNOWS OF KILIMANJARO"

[Robert Wooster Stallman taught English for many years at the University of Kansas and the University of Connecticut. He also served as editor of *The Critics Notebook, the Art of Joseph Conrad: A Critical Symposium,* and the letters of Steven Crane. In this excerpt he discusses how the interplay between Harry's interior monologues lends the story internal focus and unity.]

"The Snows of Kilimanjaro," says our biased critic, "lacks tonal and symbolic unity," but a close reading disproves that claim. "Its three planes of action, the man's intercourse with his wife, his communings with his sound, and the background of Enveloping Action, the mysterious Dark Continent, are never integrated." Well, let us examine what's what.

As the image of the leopard on Kilimanjaro's summit is integrated with the various incidents in the above recollections of Harry, so is it integrated with what Harry recollects in the subsequent italicized passage, Internal Monologue 3. It is again counterpointed against Harry as betrayer. Harry as two-timer writes the woman he loves that he cannot bear life without her, and her letter in reply is discovered by his wife: "'*Who is that letter from dear?' and that was the end of the beginning of that.*" Even that same night he wrote her from the Club he went out and picked up a girl and took her out to supper but he two-timed her: "*left her for a hot Armenian slut, that swung her belly against him so it almost scalded. He took her away from a British gunner subaltern after a row.*" Another incident he remembers has to do with artillery firing into its own troops, a metaphor of Harry destroying himself.

The fourth section of italicized reminiscences presents in contrast the happy Paris life when "*he had written the start of all he was to do. There never was another part of Paris that he loved like that,*" etc. He hadn't yet sold himself out to the rich; but he never got around to writing about the Paris he loved, nor in fact about any of the rest of his experiences.

Internal Monologue 5 follows close upon the previous recollection, and the final one of Williamson follows almost immediately. Their frequency increases towards the end of the narrative when Harry approaches death. Now he recalls the murder of an old man by a half-wit boy, whom Harry betrays. He gets the boy to aid him in packing the old man's body ("*frozen in the corral, and the dogs had eaten part of him*") onto a sled, "*and the two of you took it out over the road on skis, and sixty miles down to town to turn the boy over. He having no idea that he would be arrested. Thinking he had done his duty and that you were his friend and he would be rewarded. . . . That was one story he had saved to write. Why?*" Why Nothing sums up Harry. (Why Nothing sums up Dick Diver in *Tender Is the Night*, who likewise sold himself out to the rich.) Harry remembers "poor Julian and his romantic awe of them and how he had started a story once that began "'The very rich are different from you and me.' And how some one had said to Julian, Yes, they have more money. But that was not humorous to Julian. He thought they were a special glamorous race and when he found they weren't it wrecked him just as much as any other thing that wrecked him."

The fifth monologue spells out Harry as betrayer and links thus with the second and third italicized recollections. Again, it is a scene of death in snow and thus links with the second internal monologue. All six sections of italicized recollections present a death scene and link thus with the plight of the protagonist. Again, actions of betrayal are recurrent—in monologues number 2, 3, 4, and 5. To say that "Our attention is not called to the snow-covered peaks of Kilimanjaro until the end of the story" is to ignore these multiple interrelationships of recollected scenes with their recurrent motifs of death, deception, betrayal, and flight. The final death-dream is itself a scene of flight, flight from the Dark Continent to the House of God. The leopard made it there, but not Harry. To say that the leopard symbolism "is not part of the action and therefore does not operate as a controlling image" is to ignore the whole substance of Harry's recollected incidents; they furnish obliquely linked analogies with Harry himself and thematically they are counterpointed against the opening image of the leopard dead in the snows of Kilimanjaro's summit. Man betrays man; only the leopard is true. That opening image of the miraculous leopard operates, by my reading, as controlling and focal symbol.

—Robert Wooster Stallman, "Ernest Hemingway, A New Reading of 'The Snows of Kilimanjaro,'" *The Houses that James Built and Other Literary Studies* (Ann Arbor: Michigan State University Press, 1961): 198–199

WILLIAM VAN O'CONNOR ON HEMINGWAY'S REALISTIC WRITING

[A professor of English at the University of California at Davis, William Van O'Connor (1915–1966) also taught at New York University and the University of Liege. He was an enormously prolific and respected writer on modern poetry and literature. His works include *Sense and Sensibility in Modern Poetry, The Tangled Fire of William Faulkner, A Casebook on Ezra Pound*, and *The Shaping Spirit: A Study of*

Wallace Stevens. In this selection he compares Ernest Hemingway to Bayard Taylor, a 19th century poet, in their reactions to Africa. O'Connor shows how Hemingway's realistic writing is a reaction against the "genteel tradition" of his predecessors.]

Man, like the leopard frozen near the western summit, pushes upward. As C. C. Walcutt has put it, all reason is against the leopard being found at that height and all reason is against Harry's ambition to rise above an "aimless materialism." Whatever it was that drove the leopard up there "is the same sort of mystery as the force that keeps idealism alive in Harry." But man is in material nature. The story tells us that Harry did capitulate. He had not written the true and beautiful stories it was in his power to write. He did not live to achieve what he might have achieved. Only in fantasy does he escape from the nature that has pulled him down. In his delirium, he believes he has escaped into the mysterious beauty that Kilimanjaro symbolizes—but he has not escaped. Among the final images in the story is one almost equally vivid with the white brilliance of the mountain: "She could see his bulk under the mosquito bar but somehow he had gotten his leg out and it hung down alongside the cot. The dressings had all come down and she could not look at it." Idealism does not always win. She has an implacable foe in physical decay which succeeds in winning major victories, perhaps the major victories.

Within Taylor's vision of civilization there is a far greater assurance of strength and abiding influence than there is in Hemingway's vision. Historically, it is that the affirmations of the "genteel tradition" gave way, as everyone knows, to affirmations of a more qualified sort. Taylor, the nineteenth-century visitor to Africa, was assured that the primitive could be civilized, whereas Hemingway, the twentieth-century visitor, feels or knows that the "primitive" is a part of civilization. To develop this point much further would entail an examination of the "genteel tradition" and certain of the reactions to it. Perhaps it is sufficient to observe, once more, that Taylor, the genteel poet, superimposed a civilized order of things on a nature that the twentieth-century man sees as alien or at least as apart from him. Taylor was in awe of the mountain, but not so profoundly in awe of it as Hemingway was.

Between Bayard Taylor and Hemingway lay the breakup of the genteel tradition.

—William Van O'Connor, "Two Views of Kilimanjaro," *The Grotesque: An American Genre and Other Essays* (Carbondale: Southern Illinois University Press, 1962): 122–123

☙

RICHARD HOVEY ON AUTOBIOGRAPHICAL PARALLELS IN "THE SNOWS OF KILIMANJARO"

[A professor of English at the University of Maryland, Richard Hovey is the author of *John Jay Chapman: An American Mind*. He has also contributed extensively to journals such as the *Saturday Review, Modern Age,* and the *New England Quarterly*. In this excerpt from his book, *Hemingway: The Inward Terrain,* Hovey explores the parallels between Hemingway's life and the characterization and plot of "The Snows of Kilimanjaro."]

In none of his other short stories has Hemingway drawn between himself and the protagonist so many, so extensive, and even such specific parallels. It has been often anthologized and commented on, not so much for its art—it lacks the taut structure and incisive drama of Hemingway at his best—as for its self-revelations. Recording the last few hours of a writer dying of gangrene in the African wilderness, the narrative is virtually without action; its central conflict is a psychological one, Harry's bitter fight with himself.

Again we have a wounded hero, the gangrenous leg suggesting the long-standing castration anxiety, its stench the decay of Harry's moral nature. He admits that for years he has been "obsessed" by death. He has, in fact, been steadily destroying himself. That he neglected the thorn scratch which turns out to be fatal points to Harry's unconscious wish to die. What makes the story painful, however, is not his dying, but the bitterness and self-disgust that accompany it. For he turns upon himself a conscience which is now allied with all his destructive urges. In a mood of savage honesty,

Harry condemns himself for having thrown away his integrity as a writer and as a man.

For Hemingway the story must have been an effort to purge himself of long-accumulated guilts. No one, of course, would suggest that he has given us a full self-portrait here; it is more of a sketch drawn in a black mood. Yet in 1936 Hemingway had reasons to be dissatisfied with himself. For seven years he had given the world no novel. After *Winner Take Nothing* (1933), he had published only three short stories. These are the years when the broad-jowled grin flashes from too many news photos and the publicity makers are busy inflating the image of the brawny sportsman and bon vivant. Hemingway had been playing about in Africa and Europe and the Caribbean, drinking too much and cavorting with the rich. And he was being censured by critics on the Left and criticized for cashing in on his talents with articles to well-paying magazines. He had been through one divorce; and within four years his second marriage, to wealthy Pauline Pfeiffer, was to break up. The man who in his two most recent books had declared that the main thing for a writer was to last and get his work done appeared to be neither really lasting nor working.

—Richard Hovey, *Hemingway: The Inward Terrain* (Seattle: University of Washington Press, 1968): 127–128

SCOTT MACDONALD ON ITALICS IN "THE SNOWS OF KILIMANJARO"

[An assistant professor of American literature and film at Utica College, Scott MacDonald has written several articles on Erskine Caldwell and Ernest Hemingway in *Studies in American Fiction*, the *Journal of Narrative Technique*, and other journals. In this selection he shows how the use of italics in "The Snows of Kilimanjaro" serves to accentuate Hemingway's portrait of Harry as a failed writer.]

Critics have generally agreed that the division of "The Snows of Kilimanjaro" into italics and Roman type results in a meaningful contrast between Harry's "present ignoble situation and the memory of a more heroic past." The specific basis for the use of italics, however, causes the division of the story to have more specific implications. For one thing, the alternation of italics and Roman type keeps the reader constantly aware of the degree to which Harry has failed to fulfill his obligations as a writer. The episodes that make up the italicized sections illustrate the beauty and power of the things Harry has seen and, as a result, emphasize the loss of the fiction that Harry might have produced. The fact that some of the episodes represent numerous incidents, all of which should have become fictional material, emphasizes the extent of Harry's failure. . . .

Another implication of the use of italics in "The Snows of Kilimanjaro" involves the fact that in the final analysis the italicizing of memories is more than merely a reflection of Harry's judgement. Were the italicized episodes presented in Roman type, it would still be clear which memories Harry had saved to write and which are best forgotten. The change would in no way detract from the presentation of Harry's thinking. The fact is that in general the changes from Roman type to italics (and the breaks between the different sections) create very noticeable interruptions in the otherwise smooth process of Harry's thought, interruptions which draw the reader's attention away from Harry and toward the emphasis by the narrator which is implicit in the changes. What would really be lost if the italics were omitted is Hemingway's own emphasis that Harry should have used the episodes of the italicized sections as the raw material for fictional creation. In other words, though Hemingway does not enter "The Snows of Kilimanjaro" as an omniscient narrator in order to comment on the meaning of Harry's life, he uses italics in a way which emphasizes the fact that his protagonist has failed to fulfill his potential and that strongly confirms Harry's judgement as to which experiences he would have written about had he maintained his integrity.

One further implication of Hemingway's use of italics seems to follow. Hemingway's emphasis on the value of Harry's experiences as potential fictional material and on the protagonist's failure to capitalize on this potential makes particularly obvious the fact that at least in one sense some of the protagonist's memories *have* become fictional material. Harry's failure adequately to fulfill the duty of a writer is make clear, after all, not only by the story's catalogue of many of those specific incidents to which Harry neglected to apply his talent, but also by Hemingway's use of some of those incidents as fictional material. By drawing attention to his own act of creation through his use of italics, in other words, Hemingway subtly implies a contrast between the fate of a fictional character who has lost his moral and artistic integrity and the achievement represented by his own story, by a work of art which itself gives evidence of the fact that Hemingway's integrity as a writer remains intact. To put it another way, the achievement represented by the writing of "The Snows of Kilimanjaro" is itself the ultimate standard against which the reader can measure Harry's failure. . . .

"The Snows of Kilimanjaro" does not communicate Hemingway's vision of the artist's responsibilities, as most critics have supposed, by portraying a man who fulfills these responsibilities during the story. Instead, by presenting a man who has procrastinated the writer's job until he must be satisfied with only the dream of attaining immortality as an artist, Hemingway illustrates the kind of self-indulgence and self-deception the real artist must avoid. Hemingway's story, however, does more than portray one artist's failure. By using italics to emphasize his feeling that many of the events Harry remembers should have become the basis for artistic creation, Hemingway reminds the reader that in fact these events have been the basis for a work of art, the one the reader is reading. In other words, Hemingway contrasts Harry's failure to make the creative effort necessary for real immortality with the positive creative effort represented by "The Snows of Kilimanjaro."

—Scott MacDonald, "Hemingway's 'The Snows of Kilimanjaro': Three Critical Problems," *Studies in Short Fiction* 11, No. 1 (Winter 1974): 67–74

Works by
Ernest Hemingway

Three Stories and Ten Poems. 1923

In Our Time. 1924

The Torrents of Spring. 1926

The Sun Also Rises. 1926

Men Without Women. 1927

A Farewell to Arms. 1929

Death in the Afternoon. 1932

Winner Take Nothing. 1933

Green Hills of Africa. 1935

To Have and Have Not. 1937

The Fifth Column and The First Forty-nine Stories. 1938

For Whom the Bell Tolls. 1940

Men at War (edited and with an introduction by Hemingway). 1942

Across the River and Into the Trees. 1950.

The Old Man and the Sea. 1952

A Moveable Feast. 1964

The Snows of Kilimanjaro and Other Stories. 1964

Islands in the Stream. 1972

88 Poems. 1979

The Nick Adams Stories. 1972

Works about
Ernest Hemingway

Baker, Carlos, ed. *Hemingway and His Critics, an International Anthology*. New York: Hill and Wang, 1961.

Baker, Carlos. *Hemingway: The Writer as Artist*. Princeton, NJ: Princeton University Press, 1980.

Baker, Sheridan. *Ernest Hemingway: An Introduction and Interpretation*. New York: Holt, Reinhart and Winston, 1967.

Bakker, Jan. *Fiction as Survival Strategy: A Comparative Study of the Major Works of Ernest Hemingway and Saul Bellow*. Amsterdam: Rodopi, 1983.

Beegel, Susan F. *Hemingway's Neglected Short Fiction: New Perspectives*. Ann Arbor: University of Michigan Research Press, 1989.

Bender, Bert. "Margot Macomber's Gimlet." *College Literature* 8 (1981):12–20.

Benson, Jackson J. *Hemingway: The Writer's Art of Self-Defense*. Minneapolis: University of Minneapolis Press, 1969.

Benson, Jackson J., ed. *New Critical Approaches to the Short Stories of Ernest Hemingway*. Durham: Duke University Press, 1990.

Berryman, John. "Hemingway's 'A Clean, Well-Lighted Place.'" *The Freedom of the Poet*. New York: Farrar, Strauss and Giroux, 1976: 217–21.

Bloom, Harold, ed. *Ernest Hemingway*. New York: Chelsea House, 1985.

Brenner, Gerry. *Concealments in Hemingway's Works*. Columbus: Ohio State University Press, 1984.

Bruccoli, Matthew J. Scott and Ernest: *The Authority of Failure and the Authority of Success*. New York: Random House, 1978.

Burgess, Anthony. *Ernest Hemingway and His World*. New York: Scribner, 1978.

Burwell, Rosemarie. *Hemingway: The Postwar Years and the Posthumous Novels*. New York: Cambridge University Press, 1996.

De Falco, Joseph. *The Hero in Hemingway's Short Stories*. Philadelphia: R. West, 1983.

Donaldson, Scott. *By Force of Will: The Life and Art of Ernest Hemingway*. New York: Viking, 1977.

Donaldson, Scott, ed. *The Cambridge Companion to Hemingway*. New York: Cambridge University Press, 1996.

Elliott, Gary D. "Hemingway's 'Hills Like White Elephants.'" *Explicator* 35 (1977): 22–23.

Fenton, Charles. *The Apprenticeship of Ernest Hemingway: The Early Years.* New York: Viking, 1958.

Fleming, Robert E. "An Early Manuscript of Hemingway's 'Hills Like White Elephants.'" *NMAL: Notes on Modern American Literature* 7(1983): item 3.

Flora, Joseph M. *Ernest Hemingway: A Study of the Short Fiction.* Boston: Twayne, 1989.

Gilligan, Thomas Maher. "Topography in Hemingway's 'Hills Like White Elephants.'" *NMAL: Notes on Modern American Literature* 8:1(Spring-Summer 1984): item 2.

Gladstein, Mimi Reisel. *The Indestructible Woman in Faulkner, Hemingway and Steinbeck.* Ann Arbor: University of Michigan Research Press, 1986.

Griffin, Peter. *Less Than a Treason: Hemingway in Paris.* New York: Oxford University Press, 1990.

Herndon, Jerry A. "'The Snows of Kilimanjaro': Another Look at Theme and Point of View." *South Atlantic Quarterly* 85 (Autumn 1986): 351–59.

Hovey, Richard. *Hemingway: The Inward Terrain.* Seattle: University of Washington Press, 1968.

Howell, John, ed. *Hemingway's African Stories: The Stories, Their Sources, Their Critics.* New York: Scribner, 1969.

Hurley, C. Harold. "The Attribution of the Waiters' Second Speech in Hemingway's 'A Clean, Well-Lighted Place.'" *Studies in Short Fiction* 13 (1976): 81–85.

Johnston, Kenneth J. *The Tip of the Iceberg: Hemingway and the Short Story.* Greenwood, FL.: Penkeville, 1987.

Kerner, David. "The Foundation of the True Text of 'A Clean, Well-Lighted Place.'" *Fitzgerald-Hemingway Annual* (1979): 279–300.

Kolb, Alfred. "Symbolic Structure in Hemingway's 'The Snows of Kilimanjaro.'" *NMAL: Notes on Modern American Literature* 1 (1976): item 4.

Lynn, Kenneth Schuyler. *Hemingway.* New York: Simon and Schuster, 1987.

Madison, Robert D. "Hemingway and Selous: A Source for 'Snows'?" *Hemingway Review* 8:1(Fall 1988): 62–63.

McKenna, John J. and Marvin Patterson. "More Muddy Water: Wilson's Shakespeare in 'The Short, Happy Life of Francis Macomber.'" *American Notes and Queries* 17(1979): 73–74.

Meyers, Jeffrey, ed. *Hemingway: The Critical Heritage.* London: Routledge, 1982.

Nagel, James, ed. *Ernest Hemingway: The Writer in Context.* Madison: University of Wisconsin Press, 1984.

Reynolds, Michael. *Hemingway: The 1930s.* New York: W.W. Norton, 1997.

Reynolds, Michael S., ed. *Critical Essays on Ernest Hemingway's "In Our Time."* Boston: Hall, 1983.

Scholes, Robert and Nancy R. Comley. *Hemingway's Genders: Rereading the Hemingway Text.* New Haven: Yale University Press, 1994.

Seydow, John J. "Francis Macomber's Spurious Masculinity." *Hemingway Review* 1 (1981): 33–41.

Smith, Paul. *A Reader's Guide to the Short Stories of Ernest Hemingway.* Boston: G.K. Hall, 1989.

Spilka, Mark. "A Source for the Macomber 'Accident': Marryat's *Percival Keene.*" *Hemingway Review* 3:2 (Spring 1984): 46–49.

Unfried, Sarah. *Man's Place in the Natural Order: A Study of Hemingway's Major Works.* New York: Gordon, 1976.

Wagner, Linda, ed. *Ernest Hemingway: Six Decades of Criticism.* East Lansing: Michigan State University Press, 1987.

Waldhorn, Arthur. *A Reader's Guide to Ernest Hemingway.* New York: Farrar, Strauss and Giroux, 1972.

Weeks, Robert. *Hemingway: A Collection of Critical Essays.* Englewood Cliffs, NJ: Prentice-Hall, 1962.

Whiting, Charles. *Papa Goes to War: Ernest Hemingway in Europe 1944-45.* Marlborough: Crowood, 1990.

Whitlow, Roger. "Critical Misinterpretation of Hemingway's Helen." *Frontiers: A Journal of Women's Studies* 3 (1978): 52–54.

Williams, Wirt. *The Tragic Art of Ernest Hemingway.* Baton Rouge: Louisiana State University Press, 1981.

Young, Philip. *Ernest Hemingway: A Reconsideration.* University Park, PA: Pennsylvania State University Press, 1966.

Index of
Themes and Ideas